Positively

Uncivilized

PRAISE for books by Rena Priest

Patriarchy Blues, Winner of the 2018 American Book Award
"She brings an unapologetic acumen to some of our most ingrained cultural situations. Her poems, which are not always comfortable, are set against a lyrical, accessible backdrop, and the result is a provocative contemporary critique that will reframe perceptions and the way we see the world."
—Jenni Herrick, *Shepherd Express*

Sublime Subliminal
"Each of the poems in *Sublime Subliminal* is at once partly amusing, partly ironic, partly musical, and partly a deep reflection on the current state of the world."
—Risa Denenberg, Curator at The Poetry Cafe

Northwest Know-how: Beaches
"Entertaining, educational and highly giftable, *Northwest Know-How: Beaches* showcases the majestic, quirky, and unique beaches of the Washington and Oregon coastline through facts, history, legend, and lovely illustrations."
—Sasquatch Books

The Larger Voice: Celebrating the Work of Native Arts and Cultures Foundation Literature Fellows, edited by Rena Priest
An essential reading guide to some of the most contemporary Native literature. Consider this anthology as a place where many of our best Native speakers stand together to give us what is as essential as water: stories, prose, and poetry that will incite inspiration, community, and growth, because in this profoundly changing world, we need their words."
—Joy Harjo, NACF Board Chair & U.S. Poet Laureate

I Sing the Salmon Home: Poems from Washington State, edited by Rena Priest
"At long last salmon—the soul of the Pacific Northwest—have been given words to match the ongoing miracle of their existence. With this anthology, some of the better poets from our corner of the world show us dimensions of life, legacy, and culture that we might otherwise overlook in our rushed tumble through the years. It's a book to grow old with—and a book to share with those just learning the power of verse to change hearts and minds."
—Timothy Egan, author of *The Good Rain*

Positively

Uncivilized

Rena Priest

RAVEN
CHRONICLES PRESS
Shoreline/Seattle, Washington

RAVEN
CHRONICLES PRESS
https://www.ravenchronicles.org
Copyright © 2025 Rena Priest
Printed in the United States of America

Library of Congress Cataloging-in-Publication Data

Names: Priest, Rena, author.
Title: Positively Uncivilized, a collection of essays/Rena Priest.
Description: 1st edition | Raven Chronicles Press [2025] | Includes
    bibliographical references.
Identifiers:
    Library of Congress Control Number: 2025933390
    ISBN [paperback edition] 979-8-9914032-3-8
    ISBN [eBook] 979-8-9914032-4-5

Cover artwork © RYAN! Feddersen, *Antecedents*, 2020, commissioned by the Washington State Arts Commission in partnership with the University of Washington.
Book Design: Phoebe Bosché, using Adobe Jenson Pro (text), and
    Proxima Nova (display)
Cover Design: Scott Martin
Copy Editing: Rosalie Morales Kearns
Author's Photo (back cover): Mark Caicedo
Raven Chronicles Press
15528 12th Avenue N.E.
Shoreline, Washington 98155-6226

This book is dedicated to all the non-human communities that sustain us—to the trees for the air we breathe, to the plants and animals and creatures of the sea who give their lives so we may eat—to all the beings with whom we share a home on beautiful planet Earth.

"Civilization is the way one's own people live. Savagery is the way foreigners live."

—Octavia E. Butler, from *Seed to Harvest*, Patternist series

"**Positive,** adj. Mistaken at the top of one's voice."

—Ambrose Bierce, from *The Devil's Dictionary*

Contents

Foreword

Tao Po! I am a human being. *Tuloy!* Come share my world.

My relationship with the water and the land of the Pacific Northwest began as a child scampering around the school playground where tall cedars created the perfect setting for our story games. My friends and I pretended we were residents of a large manor and we selected certain trees as the walls of bedrooms. A stump served as our kitchen stove. We made brooms from fallen cedar boughs. I watched ants crawl up the trunk in search of sap that I could see dripping between fissures in the bark. The smell of the sea was never far away, especially when fog would roll in and shroud our manor.

My memories as an eight-year-old don't include the events outside the playground, but they still impacted me. The Vietnam War gave my parents a feeling of instability. As immigrants from the Philippines who survived World War II, they didn't want their American Dream disrupted by the suspicions they could see in the eyes of their coworkers of European descent. My father felt frustrated that he couldn't fish where he wanted even though he had a license. He didn't know about the dispute between the local Puyallup Indians and the State of Washington over treaty rights that ultimately led to the Boldt Decision upholding tribal rights to fishing areas in their traditional territory.

At the same time, children of Coast Salish tribes were suffering the loss of their history, their land, and their identity—which was, and still is, woven into the local ecosystem. It would be decades before I started to learn some of the Indigenous history of the land that I've called home for the majority of my life.

Nothing can compare, though, with lived experience.

Positively Uncivilized, by Rena Priest, provides a unique lens to view not just the natural world but also the impact of its human inhabitants, from an Indigenous perspective. Priest asserts the power of storytelling and poetry to create continuity despite the disruptions caused by settler colonialism as well as cultural and physical genocide. She is concerned with not just the past but also the present, where the same concerns for survival that their ancestors held are echoed even now in Gaza and Ukraine. Through lyric language and a vulnerability that comes from a space of determined survivance, the author calls for hope linked with action. By creating a community concerned with mutual abundance, we can learn to relate to each other and all nature as beings able to make healthy compromises for the benefit of all.

—*Rebecca Mabanglo-Mayor, MA, MFA*
Bellingham, WA, February 26, 2025

Positively

Uncivilized

Positively Uncivilized

THINK BACK, WAY BACK. What are some of the first stories you can remember being told? One of my very first memories, and possibly the reason I am who I am today, is that I remember a story. It starts out, "One fish, Two fish, Red fish, Blue fish, / Black fish, Blue fish, Old fish, New fish. / This one has a little car. / This one has a little star. / Say! What a lot of fish there are."[1] This is the story where I learned that I love words, fish, and rhyming. This is a good story.

I remember knowing that if I brought that book to my mom, she would sit beside me on the couch and do this amazing thing with her voice, like singing, which later I learned is called rhyming. Back then, I thought it was a superpower. I still think good rhymes are a superpower. All along, I have been gathering stories like this about the world and telling them to myself. Of course, not all stories are as nice as this one about the fish and the rhymes.

When we were kids, if we were being too wild, one of my parents would shout, "Quit acting like a bunch of little savages!" If we left a cup on the counter, toys on the living room floor, or a damp towel next to the hamper, we would hear, "I just cleaned this house. It looks like a bunch of dirty little Indians live here!" If we were being dumb in the grocery store or rowdy in a restaurant, they would lean over and hiss, "Act civilized," acknowledging that we weren't truly civilized, but we could at least pretend until we got to the car.

On the one hand, their name-calling was a way of taking power away from those slurs and attitudes toward our tribal identity. When your family, who loves you very much, tells you to stop acting like a savage, it becomes just a way of saying, "Check yourself." On the other hand, it's still a story about how the world sees us as dirty and positively uncivilized. Perhaps being told this story by our parents prepares us to encounter it out in the hard, white world that doesn't love us, and where the story originated and in some places is still being told around the dinner table whenever the subject of Indians arises.

This story was passed down like a curse through several generations. I believe my ancestors learned it in Catholic boarding schools, where they were taken as tiny children to be raised far from the love of their families. Something you should know about Indian boarding schools is that their creation came on the heels of the abolishment of slavery. Is it a coincidence that American elites and factories needed a new workforce, while they were taking Indian children and teaching them to be laborers and household servants? I doubt it.

When my grandmother was six, she and her sister were scooped up by government agents and taken in the back of a cattle truck to Chemawa boarding school, 300 miles from their home. My grandmother always changed the subject when I asked her about it, so I remember going to interview my grandmother's older sister about the boarding school for a writing assignment. My aunt said that when the people came from the school, it seemed going with them meant they would be better off. She said it was hard times at Lummi back then—no food, no work, no hope. The people were hungry.

In hindsight, we understand that it was hard times on the reservation for the same reasons back then as today: because the American experiment was designed to disenfranchise non-white communities by way of unfair laws, and the soul crushing abuses of racism. So Auntie told me the story of how, at the school, they were fed and taught how to sew, and they learned the bible stories; stories that convinced them the best they could do in this life was to hang their hopes on heaven in the next.

"Kill the Indian to save the man" was the slogan that set the boarding school machine into motion. It was a machine aimed at cultural genocide. But *A thing of beauty is a joy for ever*[2], so many of our beautiful cultural stories, beliefs, and customs survived.

We have a tradition at Lummi called the prayer of never-ending gratitude, where all throughout the day you are thankful for everything you encounter. My niece made a little song to help her remember. *Hy'sxw'qe, hy'sxw'qe, hy'sxw'qe, I'yes etse qwo*—It means *Thank you, thank you, thank you for the beautiful water. I'yes etse sxwiam, I'yes etse skweyel, I'yes etse neschaleche ... the beautiful story, the beautiful day, the beautiful relatives ... and on and on.*

You say thank you for everything, the birds singing at daybreak, maple seeds helicoptering down from the trees, the dance of the cottonwood shimmering silver in the breeze. You say thank you for everything and the prayer attaches itself to your heartbeat and continues throughout your life and the lives of your children and so on forever. And the word for "heart" in our language is sale. The word for "hands" in our language, is sales. So your hands do the work of your heart, which is gratitude. You put good feelings into everything you make and everything you do.

Thank you for the sunrise, thank you for the sparkles on the water, thank you for my life, thank you for the breath I make. It's a beautiful story to tell yourself about the world. As far as a way of being in the world, it signals to me the peak of refinement and civility.

So, again, I ask you to think back and try to grab hold of the first story that shaped your way of thinking about the world. What was it? Was it the Columbus story? In 1492 Columbus sailed the ocean blue... Was it the story of the First Thanksgiving? Was it the story of a man being fashioned from clay and a woman being pulled from his rib? Was it the miracle of the loaves and fishes?

You know that saying, there are two sides to every story? How often have you considered how much those stories have shaped your beliefs, your decisions, the way you see your neighbors, the way that society functions? The purpose of religious stories is to do exactly that. To act as a guidebook for how we operate. How often have you considered the other side of your most formative stories?

The Miracle of the Fishes[3]

I don't want to get into a thing
where we're arguing about whose
spiritual hero is better, but salmon
are more powerful than Jesus.

All salmon are born from virgins.
Actually, they're born right out of the earth.
Female salmon lay eggs in a riverbed.
The males come and fertilize them.
No male-female contact is made. How chaste.
Young salmon make their journey to the sea,
then return to perform the miracle of the fishes—
they spawn and die, and their nutrient-rich bodies
and blood, infused with minerals of the living sea,
feed all living beings in the salmon's natal stream.
A salmon needs only itself and its journey
to perform this miraculous feat.
This beautiful and holy communion between
salmon and all living things has been happening
longer than people have been on this planet.

On the other hand, basic transubstantiation
requires a priest, a church, an altar, a tabernacle,
an altar boy, a glass of wine, a tray of wafers,
a bell, a Bible, dogma, an initiated congregation,
the Spanish Inquisition, a history of burning women
as witches, a history of stealing and starving Indian kids,
a history of holy wars, a history of displacing and
murdering heathen Indians in the name of god,
in order to propagate a story
about a boy, born from a virgin,
whose body and blood we eat and drink
so we shall be saved.
Saved   from   what?
Not from hunger or thirst,
but from everlasting damnation in the burning
pits of hell, which, if I close my eyes to visualize,
look suspiciously like   hunger   and thirst
on this broken and burning earth.

   Ahhh, the burning pits of hell ..."Doom" is from Old English
for "Judgment." Doomsday is Judgment Day. Doomsday is a story

that belongs to Christianity, foretells the end of the world, *has a way of making this earth a temporary space.*[4] Like many prophesies, it seems to be striving toward self-fulfillment. The other side of the doomsday story, from my point of view, is the miracle of the fishes themselves—the fishes and their beautiful dance. I believe singing and dancing are the solution, if not to the world's problems, then at least to our human despair, which I believe is the cause of most of the world's problems.

We resist despair by singing and dancing—in joy or prayer. Because our eyes are set in the front of our heads, we are naturally inclined to look forward, as if into the future. But when we dance, we turn and spin and duck and jump and twirl. We see in all directions and stepping to music, we arrange time in special patterns. This is a beautiful way of changing our point of view and creating a peaceful mind which allows opportunities for solutions to enter our consciousness.

Perhaps this is why, until the American Indian Religious Freedom Act (AIRFA) was passed in 1978, it was illegal for Indians to practice our traditional spiritual songs and dances. Prior to the enacted protection of our religious freedom, the consequences of practicing our Indigenous spirituality included the destruction of ceremonial homes, confiscation of sacred items, forced removal of children, and death.

It happened in Canada too. One of my favorite Indigenous authors from across the border, Lee Maracle, says, "We died so much during the cultural prohibition days, when our singing and dancing were banned. We are thriving now because it is legal—I am sure of that." I'm sure of it too.

Together with our songs and dances are the treasures of our stories. My elder Margaret Green told a traditional story to be published and taught to tribal youth. In the preface notes of that book she says, "We had a means of oral instruction called storytelling . . . values, behavior codes, history, geography, civics, survival skills, you name it. It was all there in our stories."

I remember being a little girl, riding around my rez with my grandma and she told me the story of our mountain, Kwelshan. Soon after, we came up on Portage Island. I asked her to tell me the story of how the island came to be. In our language it's called Siles. Sile is our word for grandmother or grandfather. At low tide you can get to the island by crossing a land bridge called Sxwelisen. Anyway, I asked her to tell me the story of how the island came to be. She said, "Why don't you tell me that story?"

And I remember feeling so powerful, that the answer for how the world came to be might lie within me. I told her that Portage was once a big, beautiful whale that a jealous sorcerer turned to stone, and the whale was lonely, but everyone who loved the whale went to live there to keep her company. The birds and trees and clams and crabs all went to live there, and the water pushed a bridge there so the people could visit when the tide was out.

Imagine having that agency as a child—to be able to create the world like that and have your elder accept it as truth. This is why storytelling is a living tradition. The stories are there like magic to provide answers to our ever-changing questions. This is ancient knowledge shared by all cultures, even the Romans, that brutal empire risen from boys raised by a wolf. The word, "author" comes from the latin *auger*, which means to increase, originate, or promote. Authorship is powerful. Stories are powerful.

I remember as a child, the first poem I ever wrote was brought by my teacher to the local newspaper. They published it and the teacher clipped it out and brought it to me. I remember telling my mom that when I grew up, I would be a poet. She was like, how about a lawyer? Then, that sort of became my story. I remember sitting in Kowloon Garden when I was sixteen, having lunch with my dad, telling him all about my big plan for life, and how I would go to law school and become a lawyer.

He just ate his chow mein and then said, "Whatever makes you happy, sweetie. If you think that will make you happy, then you should do it, but only if it makes you happy. You have to do what makes you happy." That blew my mind. In a way, it was the beginning of my work to build my own identity exclusive of family expectations. The family expectation was no longer that I be rich and accomplished, but that I be happy. Discovering what makes me happy was now the work of my life. That was the start of a new story for me. It changed everything.

In our Lummi cosmology, our storytelling tradition, we have an all-powerful character called the Changer. Xaals. Xaxa means "sacred." Xaals is the sacred one. Nobody knows what the Changer looks like, because the Changer is always changing. So you never know if you're talking to Xaals at any given moment. Xaals could be anyone. Perhaps in that moment, my dad was Xaals, bringing me news of my autonomy and responsibility for my own happiness.

Sometimes I am invited to speak at events and read my poetry. Sometimes the poems I read deal with the climate crisis, and during Q & A sessions, people will ask me how I stay hopeful, knowing the extent of Deep doo doo we're in. I tell them about Xaals, and how things can change, just like the snap of your fingers.

In one of our stories about Xaals he changes gossiping little people into clams and casts them out into the mud, then covers them with the tide so he doesn't have to listen to their gossip while he's enjoying the beach. We know this must be true because when you go for a walk on the mud flats at low tide they will say, "psst!" and try to tell you a juicy secret. In another of our stories, the people have heard that Xaals is coming so they get to work preparing a feast. Soon a stranger arrives while they are cooking their food with the rays of the sun. The stranger asks, "What's going on here?"

The people answer, "Xaals is coming. We're preparing a feast. Please join us and feast when the food is ready." Turns out, the stranger is Xaals, who says, "I can see that you're kind and good people. Let me show you another way to prepare your food." And as a gift, Xaals teaches the people to make fire.

Before the missionaries came, we didn't have god the father or original sin. No woman made from the rib of a man, or anyone to tell you that you better be good because if you horse around in church, you're going to burn in hell for eternity. No. Two hundred years ago, at Lummi, nobody ever thought of that. But we had Xaals, and you never know; maybe one day you're gossiping around with your cousins at the beach and the next thing you know you've been changed into a bunch of clams out there in the mud. Or maybe you are kind to someone, and they give you a powerful gift. Stories are powerful. Not only that, but people love stories.

My auntie who I interviewed about the boarding school lived to be ninety-three. She passed away this year, and as is our tradition the family gathered to share stories about our loved one to ease our grief. One of her children shared how Auntie was a weaver. She made the most beautiful baskets and woolens, and she would travel around to gatherings and powwows and art markets—wherever they invited artists to set up their tables to sell their work. This auntie, she was really funny. Everyone loved her sense of humor. Anyway, she would always bring along some rocks that she found on the beach, and when she would set up her table, she would put out these rocks with the rest of her wares, and she would put little price tags under them.

People would look at all the beautiful handmade things she had for sale, and then ask, what's the story with these rocks? She would make up some story right there on the spot about one of the rocks and people would listen intently, then enthusiastically give her their money for the amazing rock. I wonder how many of those rocks are out there in the world with their stories, which are forever joined to the story of this funny woman at the art market. Those rocks live lives based on the story they've been given. Everything is like that.

I remember asking my grandma once why some people were given certain teachings and others were taught different things entirely. She said it's because the old people want us to work together. Each is given only one piece of the puzzle so we will learn how we fit together, and everyone has something of their own to give. We need our aunties, uncles, cousins, grandparents, to tell us these special things about the world. Every story is a gift.

I remember hearing my friend tell a story of when he was a little boy at the beach with his grandmother. He was smashing rocks against each other, and his grandmother said, "Leave the rocks alone." She told him there were beings who lived in rocks who shouldn't be bothered. He believed her, so he left the rocks alone, understanding that the earth has rights.

And this is a true belief in our storytelling tradition. There are beings in the rocks. The earth has rights.

And with that I'll retell a story that I first read under a beaded stick game set hanging on the wall of a casino, and later again in *Indian Country Today* in an article about the unearthing of a stick game set made from mastodon bones. This is a very ancient story, but it's as relevant today as ever.

*

When people first came to be on this earth—and remember the people were the last to come—we emerged naked and shivering and hungry. No fur, weak and vulnerable, the animals took pity on us and invited us into a game of chance to see who would be the hunter and who the hunted. They did this to give us a chance to share in the gift of life, to be on this planet with them. This game, *slahal*, the stick game, was played for days and days. The people were on the verge of losing it all. We were down to our very last song and our very last stick.

We were doomed for sure when one of the animals, maybe a bird, who can remember after all this time, but probably a bird, gave us a lucky song, a sacrifice so the people could keep playing. With that song, the people came back from near oblivion and won the right to be the hunters—with the understanding that we were never to forget that sacrifice of the animals and always honor their sacrifice by giving them a chance.

We entered a pact with the animals where we would never forget that we are not above them. We are in a circle with them in this great community of life, where we are interconnected and reliant on one another for the gift of being.

This is why we never take more than we need and always build a chance for escape into every trap. This is why we always say thank you when taking food. This is why we say thank you for everything every day, because we are here by the loving grace of the earth.

How positively civilized.

Notes:

1. Dr. Seuss, from *One Fish, Two Fish, Red Fish, Blue Fish,* Random House, 1960.
2. John Keats, from "Endymion, Book I," 1818.
3. *Yellow Medicine Review*, Spring 2022, "The Miracle of the Fishes."
4. Ryler Dustin . . . "has a way of making this earth a temporary space".

Defenses of Peace
in the Biosphere Reserve

I ARRIVE IN THE CASCADE HEAD BIOSPHERE RESERVE and Experimental Forest on March 1, 2024. Cascade Head is one of 28 UNESCO Biosphere Reserves in the United States. There are 309 such reserves in 41 countries worldwide. This place is special not only for its beauty but also for its distinction as the first scenic research area in the United States. It was made such by Congress in 1974 to protect and restore the region's ecological integrity. I am here as the inaugural fellow of a residency for Indigenous writers.

To better understand UNESCO's role in this biosphere reserve, I turn to their website. I find a quote from their constitution: "Since wars begin in the minds of men and women, it is in the minds of men and women that the defenses of peace must be constructed." So that settles it. I am here to construct defenses of peace—a peaceful mind responding constructively to ecological violence and the spiritual disturbances that result.

My first morning in the reserve, I wake to snow, make coffee, build a fire, and let the peaceful beauty of the place settle on me like the snow soundlessly falling into the valley below. The cabin has wall-to-wall, floor-to-ceiling windows and is perched on a hillside with a peek-a-boo view of the Salmon River, which meanders to the grand drama of the Pacific Ocean, crashing ashore less than a mile away.

The days pass, and of course, I am happy and grateful to be here, but it is an uneasy happiness, a gratitude existing on the same coin as grief. As an Indigenous person, to be in a beautiful home in a beautiful place is never a simple enjoyment. In such a house, built on the homelands of displaced peoples, colonizer violence is always standing in the corner, trying not to be noticed amid the charming architecture, architecture skillfully aimed at highlighting the landscape to make one feel as though they are a participant in nature, rather than a spectator, occasionally cheering from the luxury box.

In the most beautiful places, it is difficult to be fully at peace because I am always aware that the people who belonged to the place, who lived here because of its beauty, cared for the place for thousands of years because of its beauty, had spiritual beliefs and practices that were fused with the well-being of this place because of its innate beauty and function—I am always aware that those original people didn't simply leave because new people arrived on their shores. These places—all up and down this coast, every coast, every watershed, every nook and cranny of hospitable, desirable land—through violence, or threat of violence—were taken.

And once taken, the violence was turned from the original inhabitants to the landscape itself—ancient forests felled, salmon rivers dammed and damned, buffalo herds systematically exterminated to break down Indigenous resistance, by destroying food sovereignty to make way for privately held domesticated livestock. The introduction of livestock, agriculture, clear-cuts, mines, and factories destroyed native flora and deprived species that relied on those wild harvests so integral to survival. Each of these beings, like the original people, contributed to the balance of their homelands.

There is an assumed cultural supremacy about colonizer science that discounts knowledge rooted in a deep relationship to place. This type of science often serves the interests of extraction rather than integration. Rich men who pay for studies will never set foot in a place yet say with confidence that we primitive savages lived here in ignorance of how to cultivate our land and, therefore, have no right to it or the wealth it contains. For centuries now, they've been handing us pickaxes and plows, backhoes and hydroelectric dams—the tools of our collective destruction—and telling us to get to work becoming civilized. At the same time, they line their pockets with the spoils of our sacred homelands and the fruits of our labor. Am I angry? I am cultivating my mind in defense of peace.

The word "integrity" comes from the Latin root *integer*, meaning "intact." In this biosphere reserve where I am trying to make my mind a vehicle for peace, I must wrestle with the fact that the Western Hemisphere, and indeed the world, is no longer intact. We live in a society built on the destruction of integrity. With this knowledge, I don't know where in my mind to construct a sanctuary where a peaceful thought might live, so I read. I search for understanding, something to say. I read books on how to write, books on history, books on art. I read *Caste: The Origins of Our Discontents*, by Isabela Wilkerson, learn all the gruesome details of the American caste system. I read *Cosmic Scholar: The Life and Times of Harry Smith*, about an anthologist who recorded Indigenous spiritual songs to save them from oblivion. I read *Shapes of Native Nonfiction: Collected Essays by Contemporary Writers*, and encounter so much alchemy—courageous voices transforming the shadow of genocide into strength and places where light can once again shine.

It is hopeful but difficult. I grow sad. I call my cousin, and we chat about it. She tells me she's upset about Gaza; seeing Palestinians subjected to violence, starvation, and isolation strategies that were endured by Indigenous communities not so very long ago is triggering. "There's no help for them." She says, "Just like there was no help for our ancestors. And the news will not tell their stories the way they should be told."

I think about how the genocide in Gaza began with the burning of their ancient olive groves. We end our phone call trying to encourage each other, but I am still sad. My cousin's talk of Gaza makes me recall a recent breakfast with a family member and his wealthy girlfriend. The crisis in Palestine came up in our conversation, and the woman said, "It's just terrible. They should be allowed to have a reservation too. Everyone deserves somewhere to live." Then she changed the subject to conversation better paired with her Bloody Mary. My husband watched to see if I would keep the peace. Of course, I would keep the peace. What could possibly be gained in shit stirring? Besides, she got it half right: *Everyone deserves somewhere to live.*

There is no need for a whole genocide right now. There was no need for one beginning in 1492 and continuing on for hundreds of years. There is no need for the burning of olive groves, the extermination of buffalo and salmon, the eradication of biodiversity in favor of domesticated, monetizable monoculture.

There never has been a need for it. "Since wars begin in the minds of men and women, it is in the minds of men and women that the defenses of peace must be constructed." Everyone deserves somewhere to live: people, fish, birds, wildflowers, trees and bugs. Spaces for holistic habitation should be preserved and protected, and this effort by UNESCO is beautiful.

Still, it would be better if we as a species didn't condemn healthy ecology to such oppressively small quarters. It would be better if the biosphere reserve were the big one, the original homelands, the whole planet. To draw a little boundary around a space and declare it **Nature: Preserved** is like the legendary king trying to carpet his kingdom to protect his delicate feet rather than wear shoes. It's good to make the initial step toward protecting something, but as my mind strives toward peace, it keeps returning to an obvious conclusion. We must try to find a way back to integration, integrity, a way of being intact. How? I think it begins with belief. I believe there are answers in ancestral knowledge. I'm not talking about this in a woo-woo way. I'm talking about it from a standpoint of Indigenous knowing.

I was listening to a neuroscientist talk about gut reactions. She explained how our gut is connected to the nervous system and responds when we know something intuitively. The interviewer asked her, "What is intuition?" She said that we have a limited amount of access to memory but everything we encounter is stored somewhere in our brains even if we can't easily retrieve it. All our accumulated knowledge and experience is there, and when we must make a decision with limited information, our intuition kicks in. We have a feeling, a physical feeling, about what needs to be done. She said this accumulation of information and awareness of the world gained through experience is the reason older people have a stronger sense of intuition.

In my tribal community, elders are revered for this reason. What if honing intuition through accumulating knowledge and experience works the same way over generations? Imagine living in a place for your whole life. You would learn its patterns, what grew where, when the tide turned, what drew the fish and game, and how to harvest so that more would return next time; you would feel safe and connected to your surroundings.

Now, imagine your DNA thriving in those landscapes and waterways, forming symbiotic, spiritual, and physical relationships there for ten, fifteen, twenty thousand years. You would have connections to that place that newcomers couldn't replicate. The food there would be tied to your gut flora and those special brain-body pathways for instinct and intuition would be supported by the food you ate, the water you drank.

In search of the science of integration, I turn to the oral histories of my ancestors. Their brilliant, integrated worldview is soothing in the perfect sense it makes. For example, in Lummi lore, it is said that if we treat the salmon with respect, they will "travel from their longhouse, the smoke of which is like a rainbow, and journey to the fishing sites to be food for the people." I wonder what kind of fire makes smoke like a rainbow. How does the fire of the salmon people burn? I don't know, but its power is restorative.

In old Lummi culture, there is a belief in a world under the water that mirrors our own. It is upside down. Tiny things are big, and big things are tiny. Smoke is made of rainbows. Here in our world, rainbows come when the sun shines after the life-giving rains. A rainbow is a symbol of renewal. So, smoke made of rainbows is a symbol of new life, and the fire of the salmon people is not destructive but creative.

When the salmon return, they are the spark of life that will carry us into a new season. A spark that finds fuel is the beginning of fire. An electrician once told me that a high-voltage electrical arc (essentially a really big spark) can be as hot as the surface of the sun. The sun, of course, is a star. A star, of course, is a fire. Are we not made of the stars? Are we not also fire? Yes. We are. Fire consumes. Fire destroys. People consume. People destroy. But fire also purifies and makes space for new life, so it is both destructive and creative. We have our place here, just as the salmon people have their smoke rainbows in the sea. ("Did you hear about the rainbow who got in trouble? It had to go to prism. It was a light sentence.")

If you use sound waves to burst a bubble under water, it will expire in a flash of light, light that by its nature is a rainbow. The phenomenon is called "sonoluminescence." Science can't fully explain it. Another phenomenon that science can't fully explain is called wave-particle duality. It is studied via what's known as the double-slit experiment. In the experiment, light behaves as a wave unless observed, in which case it acts as discrete particles. Is it childlike to try to understand this inexplicable fact by saying that the universe, at the level of particles, is conscious?

In my culture, it is not unusual to go and express gratitude and prayer to the water. The water is conscious. Like light, it behaves as both particles and waves. Why would light not be the same? It is the same. In my ancestral language, the word for "river" is also the word for the Milky Way, a river of light in the sky, a river of billions of burning suns. It continues that idea of the mirror world under the waves, the multi-layered nature of existence. Everything is connected. The ancestors understood this deeply.

A friend of mine shared a story about his visit to a national forest in Oregon. The tour host was a geologist who gave a presentation on what he calls the "mythic dimensions" of his research, which otherwise is rooted in what he calls the "hard-ass science" of "geophonics, biophonics, and anthropophonics —sounds made by different components of the world." The talk overviewed ecological interconnection through sound, and how a fish in need of a home can send out a signal, which is received by the forest and the roots of trees, which may respond by felling a tree over the stream in exactly the right place to slow the current and make the stream habitable for the fish. Spawning salmon bring nutrients from the ocean into the forest, so salmon have symbiotic relationships with the trees and the underground fungal networks that connect them.

I don't know if this is why the tree would respond the way it did, but what this story seems to want to teach is a fundamental understanding of one of my favorite features of reality: that the right combination of wishing, need, and expression can find an audience with a conscious and benevolent universe.

That the universe, in its infinite intelligence, with the infinite connections between the fires that shine above and those that glimmer below, will seek balance, will hear a request, and find a way to make it so. Remembering this good teaching about having faith in the benevolence and wisdom of nature, I have finally constructed a defense of peace in my mind.

FISH OUTLAWS
Reflections on the Criminalization of Indigenous Fishers and Imagining Just Futures

1. The Long Fight for Treaty Rights

ACADEMIC PAPERS, NEWS ARTICLES, AND BOOKS have been published, movies have been made, and songs have been sung about the Fish Wars, the infamous struggle that resulted in the landmark case, *United States v. State of Washington*. Here, at the 50th anniversary of the Boldt Decision, we are presented with an opportunity to look back and see what has transpired between that historically significant moment and the present.

It's helpful to recall that the struggle to have our treaty rights honored didn't begin with the arrests, beatings, and confiscation of personal property during the civil rights era. By the time the movement leading to *United States v. State of Washington* got underway, the state's unjust activities to deprive Indigenous peoples of treaty rights had been going on for over a century.

With the perfection of the canning process in the 1880s, salmon came to be seen as a valuable commodity. In the 1890s, non-Indigenous fishers annually took 40 million pounds of salmon out of the Columbia River alone. But the absolute devastation came in the 1930s with the construction of hydroelectric dams. In some instances, dams built throughout the region were responsible for leading to the total extinction of salmon runs in a river.

> "As long as the rivers run, as long as the tide flows, and as long as the sun shines, you will have land, fish, and game for your frying pans and timber for your lodges."
> —Isaac Stevens, Governor of Washington Territorial

In Whatcom County, the Lummi tribe fought a landmark case against violations of our treaty rights and the abuses leveled against our fishers by the cannery at Point Roberts. In 1897

William Brinker, U.S. Attorney for Washington, filed suit against the Alaska Packers Association on behalf of the Lummi tribe to restore rights to our fishing grounds. Judge Hanford was given the case and ruled against the provisions of treaty rights for the third time in five years.

During the case, tribal fishers testified to being threatened by the defendant with a revolver if they didn't move off their fishing claims. When they left, John Waller tore down their fishing shacks and used the timber to construct his cannery. He then installed fish traps, which depleted fish stocks to the point where they were no longer profitable for tribal reef netters who had been fishing the site for more than 4,000 years.

> "H.B. Kirby, who was then in the employ of the defendant Association, came to the shack occupied by me on the beach and ordered me to leave and stayed around until I left. He threatened me with injury if I did not leave."
> —Old Polen, Lummi fisher

In 1913 the Lummi tribe was in the judicial system again when tribal member Harry Price allowed himself to be arrested to make a test of treaty fishing rights. Lummi won the case, but the enraged state fish and game commissioner asserted that he would continue to arrest Lummi fishermen. Lummi sought an injunction against the commissioner to prohibit continued arrests. The injunction was not enforced, and the commissioner continued his harmful actions.

In 1915 Lummi retaliated by conducting a citizen's arrest on a group of Austrians fishing in Lummi waters. The poachers were held at an undisclosed Lummi residence until news of the arrest reached the Oval Office. President Wilson, wishing to avoid international conflict, instructed the state fish commissioner to cease harassment of Lummi fishers. The Austrians were released, but antagonism of Lummi fishers continued for decades to follow.

March 30th of 2022 marked 80 years since *Tulee v. Washington*, a court decision handed down in 1942 that would leave "the state with the power to impose on Indians equally with others, as necessary for the conservation of fish." But it was felt and expressed by Indigenous fishers that the state used the term "conservation" as a weapon against them to criminalize their way of life. The harvest of the commercial fishery and loss of salmon to hydroelectric dams is evidence of it.

> "You know, when you speak of conservation, if they're going to conserve, they should start conserving out in the outer waters, particularly in the Puget Sound after the fish leave the straits of Juan De Fuca. You can go out here in the Puget Sound when they're fishing out there and find numerous commercial boats, and their take, one purse seine boat out there in the sound, can take probably more fish in one day than our whole group can take in one season. There's various ways that the Indian has always practiced conservation. This was done almost automatically. Not only did they allow an escapement, but elements of nature provide for escapement."
> —Al Bridges, father of Nisqually activist Valerie Bridges

There are stories in our oral histories of Indigenous peoples recalling the devastation of seeing salmon piled up dead at the base of dams and similar stories of salmon piled up dead on the shoreline because the canneries didn't want them or couldn't process them fast enough.

The canneries must have realized that it wasn't a good look to have their misuse of the fish washing up on shore, so they began piling the unused salmon up in great heaps on a barge and sending it offshore to rot. Knowing this, imagine the burn of injustice to be shut out and criminalized for practicing your lifeway on the grounds of conservation.

Sampson Tulee, who brought the court case, *Tulee v. Washington*, was a Yakima tribal member. At the same time that Tulee's struggle for fishing rights was taking place, the neighboring Wanapum tribe was facing relocation from their fish-curing village to make way for the Hanford Nuclear Reservation.

Today, the Hanford nuclear reactor sits along the stretch of river where the tribal spiritual leader Smoholla once lived. The land around Hanford is more contaminated by nuclear waste than any other site in North America. The reactor was built in the early 1940s to produce the plutonium used in the bombs dropped on Hiroshima and Nagasaki.

"Back in the '40s, the people who lived at Hanford were driven off there and had the land taken from them. My people had a village up there. We had sheds up there for curing salmon, and then in 1943 they moved all the people out of there"
—David Sohappy (Wanapum fisher)

Twenty years later, in 1967, *State v. McCoy* would come along and justify the state's imposition of "reasonable and necessary regulations" on tribes. These impositions would be made in violation of the treaties. Days before Christmas in 1963, tribal members staged a protest at the Washington state capital in Olympia. They carried signs that read "No salmon—No Santa." After inviting them in and hearing their complaints, Governor Rosellini dismissed them, saying, "Nice to hear your problems. Come back again."

Early in 1964, the group founded Survival of the American Indian Association to work toward having their treaty fishing rights honored as the result of uncompromising civil disobedience. Another decade would pass, and tribes would still be in the fight to have the treaties honored. In 1974 U.S. Attorney Stan Pitkin filed suit on behalf of tribes.

"The biggest thing that ever happened in our time was we had an encampment on the Puyallup River; there must have been three or four hundred of us and our kids and everything—we had a fire, and we had an encampment. Everyone was living there, and we were fishing on the Puyallup River. They gassed us that day. They gassed all of us. They gassed the US Attorney, Stan Pitkin. We'd been begging Stan Pitkin and all the US attorneys to take our case, you know, 'the state of Washington is beating

us up every night and every day there, over treaty rights, and you guys haven't done a thing.' Well, when they got gassed, he took the case, and that's what happened in US v. Washington."
—Billy Frank Jr., Nisqually environmental activist

On June 4, 1975, Judge George Hugo Boldt handed down his decision honoring the tribes' right to 50 percent of the salmon catch available for harvest after an allotted amount had been reserved for conservation. But the fight to protect the fishery and our harvest rights was far from over. Though the Boldt Decision was handed down in 1975 and finalized in 1979, tribes in the interior part of Washington state were still fighting to have their treaty rights honored and were facing the backlash of those who disagreed with the decision.

2. The Catch

BY THE TIME THE BOLDT DECISION came around in 1974, regional fisheries were already experiencing a steep decline. After a century of overfishing by non-treaty commercial fishers, the destruction of salmon habitat, and the installation of dams on salmon-bearing streams, some runs were on the brink of collapse. Policy-makers who opposed the Boldt Decision now saw tribal fishers as the perfect scapegoat to bear the onus for the declining runs. Despite and perhaps because of their small numbers and recent arrival on the commercial scene, tribal fishers became easy targets for the frustrations of non-treaty fishers who now had to share an already depleted harvest.

Eight years after the Boldt Decision was finalized, on June 17, 1982, Wanapum spiritual leader David Sohappy and his son were arrested in a raid at Cooks Landing on the Columbia River. They were brought in for selling salmon out of season. Sohappy was charged with selling 317 salmon, while his son was charged with selling 27 fish to undercover operatives. The 344 fish that the Sohappys were convicted of selling were worth about $10,000. This income was used to support an extended family of about 20 people.

Initially, they had been charged for illegally harvesting 40,000 fish that had disappeared above the Bonneville Dam. It was later discovered that the fish had gone elsewhere to spawn due to fluoride in the water that aluminum mills along the river had dumped. Despite this finding, the Sohappys were sentenced to five years in prison.

"In 1982, shortly before the massive raid on the Sohappy family camp, Wayne Lewis of the National Marine Fishery Service wrote a letter to the Interior Department, questioning the Sohappys' right to be there, and in 1983, shortly after David was found guilty, the Secretary of the Interior was urged to bring an eviction action. I think it is beyond dispute that the evictions are tied to the entire salmon scam prosecution. It's an effort to push the Sohappy family, first out of the Columbia River and then off Cooks Landing."
—Thomas Keefe, Jr., defense attorney

Another likely reason for the harsh sentence was David Sohappy's history as a treaty rights activist. In 1968 he was arrested and won a landmark case, *Sohappy v. Smith*, establishing the precedent that the state must provide valid proof of a conservation activity to interfere with tribal fishing.

Though the media portrayed Sohappy as the ringleader of a criminal fishing operation, he was protesting on behalf of his religious freedoms. His activism was deeply rooted in his traditional spiritual beliefs.

"They say I'm crazy, but the salmon have to be worshiped. The salmon only come back to the people that worship them. You got the federal laws, then you got the international laws, then you got the constitutional laws, then you got state laws, then you got tribal laws that the Indians got to deal with. A long time ago, the Indians had their own unwritten laws. They never broke it. To break it was to be the end of him."
—David Sohappy, member of the Confederated Tribes and Bands of the Yakama Nation

Sohappy was the great-grandnephew of the Wanapum tribal spiritual leader Smoholla, who carried forward their traditional belief that wisdom comes in dreams. He shared a prophetic dream that the future would bring great destruction and told his people that they must continue to live along the river and continue fishing because only those who practiced the old ways would survive. When the U.S. government passed a law insisting that all Indians become farmers, Smoholla said, "It's not a good law that would take my people away from me and make them sin against the laws of god. You ask me to plow the ground. Shall I take a knife and tear my mother's bosom? Then when I die, she will not take me to her bosom to rest. You ask me to dig for stone. Shall I dig under her skin for bones? Then when I die, I cannot enter her body to be born again."

In 1978 President Carter passed the American Indian Religious Freedom Act. In some ways, the Sohappy case was a test of the American will to uphold its own laws on behalf of religious freedom. During the Sohappy trials, the beliefs he was willing to go to prison to defend were mocked by Assistant U.S. Attorney Stephen Schroeder, who said, "Mr. Sohappy's religion, if it is his religion, is a very convenient one, it seems to me, if it justifies this massive buying/brokering of illegal fish that he did."

Sohappy was released from prison two years into his sentence, but not before suffering a stroke. U.S. Senator Daniel Inouye intervened on behalf of the Sohappys, saying, "The more I studied the case, the more it became obvious to me that something was wrong."

Despite the U.S. Attorney's skepticism, there is a documented history of tribal commerce in alignment with spiritual laws. Trading fish for a living was a traditional spiritual way of living. Trade meetings provide tribes an opportunity to visit and enjoy news from neighboring communities. Tribes from the coast would often travel inland to trade with those who fished on the Columbia River, where fish were renowned as some of the region's best.

The size of a salmon is related to the distance it travels to spawn. Before the Grand Coulee Dam was installed, Columbia

River salmon traveled all the way into Canada. The Wanapum and Yakima tribes fished what were once called summer hogs, because these fish could grow to be as big as a hog. This form of trade was, in fact, part of a sacred way of life.

"I don't think there's any question of racism behind what happened to David Sohappy and his son and the other defendants. It happened to Sohappy because he's inconvenient and because he's an Indian."
—Phil Stanford, American journalist

The criminalization of Indigenous fishers has been only one of many strategies enacted by the state to erode treaties and undermine federal obligations to tribes for the millions of acres ceded to make way for white habitation. In addition to scapegoating tribal fishers as the reason for stock depletions, the government also made tribes accountable for fish harvested under the guidelines of *United States v. State of Washington* by mandating the operation of hatcheries to replenish the stock.

Some tribal members see hatcheries as interfering with nature's wisdom and the salmon's sacred circular journey. But others see hatcheries as a means of profit, and here is another way the Boldt Decision impacted the covenant between tribes and salmon: In acknowledging and restoring our rights to be out on the water, under colonial law, tribal fishers entered the arena now as commercial fishermen. In my teens, I was allowed to participate in the commercial fishery for a season. After the net opened onto the deck, my job was to sweep fish by the flopping thousands into the ice box. I remember looking down into the box and feeling an overwhelming sense of grief wash over me as the hundreds of fish at the top of the piles took their last breaths, their mouths and gills opening and closing.

A crew member asked, "What's the matter?" On the verge of tears I said, "It's just so much death." He replied, "That's not death! That's money!" And I never forgot how this statement contrasted with what I had been taught as a child, about how the salmon were sacred and were to be thanked and treated with reverence.

With the Boldt Decision, we were thrust into capitalism and the marketplace. We came to see the gift of the salmon not as a sacrifice supporting an ancient and sacred relationship but as a cash stream to which we were entitled, not by nature, but by federal obligation. When we agreed to interfere with their journey by raising salmon in hatcheries, this too is when we let colonial laws dupe us into giving up our sacred covenant with the salmon in exchange for a way out of the crushing poverty that had long been imposed by a socioeconomic system designed to keep indigenous peoples in a constant state of financial vulnerability.

In 2019 Patagonia released a movie called *Artifishal*, aimed at raising awareness about how hatcheries harm wild salmon populations. However, the documentary paints hatchery tribes in a negative light, and while it's true Patagonia has a stated mission to protect nature, let's be clear, Patagonia is a corporation, and the reason they want to save the wild salmon is not entirely altruistic. It's not just for the bears or eagles or orcas. Nor is it to uphold treaty obligations to tribes. No, it's so they can process a wild and rare product to sell in a niche fine-food market.

Patagonia's attack on hatchery tribes could signal a new way of scapegoating tribes to let state and local governments off the hook for obligations to environmental concerns raised by their constituents. The deficit in public understanding of treaty obligations and laws makes it essential to look at why some tribes are hatchery tribes and why it's no simple thing for us to simply get rid of the hatcheries. In addition to mitigating tribal involvement in the fishery, hatcheries were implemented to justify dams. The powers that be, way back as early as the 1800s, said, if we can just produce salmon in hatcheries, then they don't need to go upstream to spawn, and we can go ahead and put this dam right here.

Are we surprised that during the Industrial Revolution, fish would be raised in hatcheries and forced to swim in circles for maximum output, while little Indian children were taken from their homelands to be raised in factory schools and forced to march in circles until they could punch clocks for maximum output?

Okay, but now we know boarding schools were cultural genocide and the government has stopped the brutal practice of taking children from their families to "Kill the Indian to save the man." The salmon are not so lucky. While science can prove that pumping 5 billion hatchery fish into the wild harms wild salmon runs, it's still not seen as necessary to shift course. But it isn't tribes behind this behemoth worldwide hatchery campaign, as Patagonia might have you believe. It is federal, state, and local governments together with hydroelectric power companies across the globe. There have been hundreds of millions of dollars, perhaps billions, put into selling the public on the idea of hatcheries.

It bears repeating that when the Boldt Decision came around in 1975 restoring tribal treaty rights to the fishery, one of the conditions was that tribes would take action to put back what they harvested. Hatcheries were an idea imposed on tribes. Some elders opposed it, but the science at the time assured the people that it would help the salmon and benefit tribes in the funding it would provide.

The government spent millions of 1970s dollars to convince us of the soundness of their science and then millions more to install these operations in our homelands. At Lummi, they funded an operation called the Lummi Island School of Aquaculture (LISA), where they trained tribal members in hatchery operations and taught a curriculum that affirmed the soundness of the science behind aquaculture. The state then funded the construction of two hatcheries. Tribal leaders, together with Marlon Brando were invited onto *The Dick Cavett Show* to espouse the brilliant ecological benefits of hatcheries.

Despite the science outlining the destructive impact of hatchery fish on wild salmon, the system is still in full swing. On May 17, 2023, the Lummi Nation issued a press release announcing an award of funding from the state capital budget that put forward more than $10 million for hatchery production and restoration at Lummi facilities. Is it any wonder we have tribal council members and tribal

Endangered Species Administration directors saying, "Hatchery fish are treaty fish"?

3. Vision for a Just Future

A TREATY ENTERED INTO by the United States Government puts forth the supreme law of the land. Therefore, it's necessary to place the treaty and tribal priorities at the forefront when undertaking matters of salmon. As onboarding tribes into the aquaculture industry was an investment, so must be onboarding tribes into a more scientifically sound way of salmon restoration. We must be funded. Considering what was taken from tribes and the ecological well-being of our homelands—which in Washington State over the last 200 years has been hundreds of billions in profits from the fishery, canning, hydroelectric, and finally, the aquaculture industry—funding tribal stewardship can be seen only as a necessary step toward reconciliation.

Vilifying us in documentaries is not the answer, nor is it wise to entrust corporations with the care of our most precious planet. No matter how philanthropic its mission, by its nature, a corporation is most beholden to the bottom line. If community interest groups and policymakers prove to be more interested in scapegoating tribes than providing more scientifically sound salmon restoration opportunities, that is a mistake, and as history demonstrates, the planet's health suffers when tribes are excluded from participation in decision-making regarding ecological stewardship.

For Washington lawmakers, envisioning a just future for salmon and tribes requires an act of imagination, while for tribes, the vision for ecological justice is an act of remembrance. We remember what life was like before colonial laws and activities depleted fish runs and dismantled ancient sustainable lifeways. In their Declaration on the Rights of Indigenous Peoples, the United Nations recognizes "that respect for indigenous knowledge, cultures, and traditional practices contributes to sustainable and equitable development and proper management of the environment."

For example, on the fifth anniversary of California's apology to Native Americans, the Shasta Nation won the largest victory of land repatriation in California history: 2,800 acres were returned to the nation, resulting in more than 300 miles of restored salmon habitat. This means healthier ecology for the whole region. When tribes win, everyone wins.

Before the treaty was signed at Point Elliott, tribes gathered for several days to talk over what they would ask for. The ancestors knew that as long as there were fish, trees, and clean water, the people would be okay. They did what they could to ensure the survival of the people by asking for assurances of access to fishing, hunting, and harvesting grounds, and promises were made to quell their concerns.

When I was invited to write a poem to open the joint legislative session in 2023, I was told that the theme would be "A vision for equality in 2023." It seemed important to me to state what should be obvious: there is no equality without acknowledging that we live in an ecosystem—are interdependent organisms, reliant on the health of the whole. That despite what was promised by men with pens seeking signatures to justify their crimes against equality, the only way to promise eternal access to fish, game, and forests is to take care of them.

These Abundant and Generous Homelands

Warm at home, in the long cold days of winter,
how and why should it trouble our thoughts,
that eternal question of the haves and have-naughts?
We are not thoughtless or hard of heart.
We give what's fair, do our part,
and the privileges we claim as our share,
those we reserve without reservation—
Perhaps even unaware of our good fortune.
Perhaps, never having *troubled deaf heaven*
with my bootless cries,[1] we walk well-heeled

through our blessed lives with ease,
or maybe we stride with shrewd purpose
in shoes made for long days of toil on our feet.
You have yours, and I have mine, and aren't most of us
just trying to get by? But still, the hungry—
they are always with us and isn't the worry always
that if we pause our labor too long to care too much
that we shall be counted among them?

How can equality be anything but a utopian dream
for those whose history and legends tell only
of statesmen and kings and whose concerns
are less and less over the justness of wars
as much as they are for the accumulation
of more, more, more?

Yet we live on lands where equality bloomed once before,
when Indigenous nations lived by beliefs
and followed ancient laws that said an orca whale
and a cedar tree are sovereign, sentient beings
with inviolable rights, just like you and me.
Those beliefs are not childlike or primitive.
They are the blueprint for a just and fair society,
which for Native nations is not a vision but a memory.

That sublime belief in the wisdom and goodness
of the giving earth, is not so elusive, is not
a birthright exclusive to tribes. Yes, it's mine,
but it's yours too, if you want it. If you want it,
you must tell new stories—true stories
on which to build new beliefs—true beliefs,
in the interconnection and value of all living things.

The supremacy of man is only fiction.
This is the secret every river knows, for water rises
and falls, and in a circle, eternally flows
from the cloud to the mountain

through the valley to the sea. Thus, is a circle,
a balanced, perfect, and natural state of being.
And who are we to interrupt it?
We do so at our peril.

When the forest burns, our eyes burn,
and our hearts fill with ashes. And when streams
are dammed and wanting of salmon,
doesn't our blood also want of vitality?
This is the folly of hierarchy, with man at the top.
We reap the fruit of inequity.
A harvest of terrible hunger.
Now is the hour of our reckoning,
a moment of dire lack.

Though unrehearsed,
we must summon the courage
and the will to act, to assure our children
a better path forward. And when we look back,
will we see that in fact
we were not recovering from natural disasters,
rather, we were the great disaster
from which nature must recover?

With hindsight for eyes, we must sail toward
a beautiful vision: an era that is trying but hopeful,
demanding, but healthy, whole, and equitable?
We will be steadfast in our course, carried
by the winds of change, into a more balanced way
of being, for while free will is at the whim
of our human nature, nature loves balance,
and so, our nature is humane.

To repair this world we must recall a time
when we did not have the things we think, we need
but had the whole living earth for free.

"As long as the rivers run, as long as the tide flows,
and as long as the sun shines, you will have land, fish and
game for your frying pans, and timber for your lodges."[2]

These are the promises only the earth can make
and only in exchange for our reverence,
and yet these were the promises made by a man,
in exchange for a treaty
on which the foreign state was founded
here, in these sacred homelands
where once, the call of eagles resounded,
resplendent from the tops of towering cedars,
where none went hungry
when salmon were running,
in clear, cool waters,

these abundant and generous homelands
were given in exchange for the promise
of a world we could live in
a world that would keep giving,
to all in common,
for as long as the rivers run.

4. Timeline

BEFORE COLONIZATION

Food in abundance—clams, oysters, mussels, crab, whale,
steelhead trout, salmon, halibut, smelt, candlefish, camas root,
berries, native vegetables, hops, deer, elk, bear, mountain goat,
etc. Diverse harvesting and food preservation technologies: i.e.
spearfishing, gill netting, weir fishing, reef netting, whaling, and
jacklighting. Complex regional trade system:

> "Because the food and other trade items were so plentiful, people
> had to become specialists in order to produce goods for trade.
> One could not simply smoke salmon because everyone

did. Rather, the different villages had to develop specialty items that would be coveted by other tribes in order to participate in the trade."
—Vine Deloria, Jr., author, Standing Rock Sioux Tribe

First European arrival

1782: First indication of European presence (Nootka Sound, Cook expedition). Smallpox plague sweeps through Puget Sound. Disease strikes twice more by 1850, reducing Native populations by nearly 80 percent.

1788: Captain Gray's expedition to Chinook territory, what is now the Columbia River.

> *"I was received at my landing by an old chief who conducted me with Mr. Smith [another officer] to his house; seated us by a good fire; offered us to eat and drink of the best the house afforded; which was dried fish of various sorts, roasted clams and mussels. Water was our drink, handed in a wooden box with a large sea clam shell to drink out of; the chief's son attended me, opened my clams, roasted my fish, and did various other kinds of offices in which he was pleased to engage. After this entertainment we were greeted with two songs, in which was frequently repeated words, 'Wakush Tiyee a winna' or 'Welcome traveling chief.'"*
—John Hoskins, officer on the Gray expedition

While the chief was busy entertaining the officers of the ship, a crewman killed a tribesman. The ship then fled the area.

1792: British expedition under Captain George Vancouver, in which islands, straits, and mountains are given the names they are currently known by.

1805–08: Forts St. James, McLeod, Fraser, and George are built.

1811: John Jacob Astor builds Fort Astoria as fur trade increases in the region.

1818: The United States and Great Britain make a ten-year agreement that citizens of either country could settle what was then known as the Oregon Territory.

1820s–40s: Relative peace is enjoyed between Natives and the immigrant population.

1835: Jason Lee is the first missionary (Methodist) sent to the region, establishing a mission in the Willamette Valley near the Oregon coast.

1838: Puget Sound Agricultural Company is established.

1843: The Great Migration along the Oregon Trail begins.

1852: Word arrives among tribes of the massacres of many Californian tribal villages by miners. Tribes brace for onslaught of new immigrants.

1853: Washington Territory is created.

TREATIES AND RESERVATIONS

1854: Treaty negotiations begin. Governor Isaac Stevens insists on using an old Chinook trade jargon to explain the provisions of treaties. The jargon consisted of fewer than 300 words, including Indian words, some English, and some French.

> *"I could talk the Indian languages, but Stevens did not seem to want anyone to interpret in their own tongue, and had that done in Chinook. Of course it was utterly impossible to explain the treaties to them in Chinook. Stevens wanted me to go into the war but I wouldn't do it. I know it was his bad management that brought on the war, and I wouldn't raise a gun against*

those people who had always been so kind to us when we were weak and needy."
—Owen Bush, treaty session attendee

"Governor Stevens was intoxicated and unfit for transacting business while making these treaties."
—Ezra Meeker, author

1855: Lack of clarity in treaty provisions leads to conflicts exacerbated by misleading information printed in newspapers. Unlawful land grabs result in the displacement of several Native villages by squatters.

1856: Outraged tribes attack the settlement of Seattle and are put down by shelling from warships in the harbor. Conflicts ensue over the next three years, in which Stevens encourages the fight against the Indians by organizing "volunteer" companies, which were groups of bandits that raided tribal villages.

1860: Agents implement policies dictating that "all Indians" be farmers. Such policies were meant to ensure the acceptance of white lifeways.

"The land on the Tulalip, Madison, and Swinomish is of such a poor quality that it affords but little encouragement to the Indians to follow farming as a business, for with the exception of a few small sails or marshes it is high and gravelly, and thickly covered with a dense growth of fir, cedars, and spruce. It requires an immense amount of labor to clear a few acres and even when in a fit condition for planting the yield is so small that it is truly discouraging, and would tax the continuity of a more industrious and determined people."
—From an annual report by the Indian agent at Tulalip (1879)

1879: The first tribal council is established at Puyallup. By the mid-1880s nearly every reservation has its own council, police force, and a system of tribal courts.

Fish Outlaws

1889: Washington is admitted as a state. Immediate questions of jurisdiction over tribal lands and resources are raised between the state and federal government.

1892: In a case brought against a Makah whaler, Judge Hanford makes a ruling reversing the provision of treaty rights that had been upheld for over 40 years.

1896: Judge Hanford rules against the Yakima using the arguments he used in deciding the Makah case.

1897: William Brinker, U.S. Attorney for Washington, files suit against the Alaska Packers Association on behalf of the Lummi tribe to restore rights to fishing grounds at Point Roberts. Judge Hanford is given the case and rules against the provisions of treaty rights for the third time in five years.

1905: The Yakima case is appealed to the Supreme Court. The court rules in favor of the Yakima.

> "From 1905 on, Indians would be in court almost continuously trying to defend their fishing rights against the intrusions of white fishermen."
> —Vine Deloria, Jr., author

1913: Harry Price (Lummi) allows himself to be arrested in order to make a test of treaty fishing rights, which the state fish commissioner agrees will settle the question once and for all. Lummi wins the case, but the outraged commissioner announces that he will continue to arrest Lummi fishermen. Lummi instructs their lawyer to seek a permanent injunction against the state fish commissioner, to forbid continued arrests. He escaped the injunction and persisted in the harassment of Lummi fishers.

1915: Lummi retaliates by arresting a group of Austrians fishing in Lummi waters. Word reaches the Oval Office. The president, wishing to avoid international conflict, instructs that the state fish commissioner cease harassment of Lummi fishers, but antagonism resumes in decades to follow.

1934: A case filed in the late 1920s is decided against tribes. The suit was filed when outraged tribes banded together against the federal government for failure to fulfill treaty requirements, mainly in regard to fishing rights which were being denied while the fish harvesting practices of non-Natives went unchecked.

> "At the headwaters of a short creek emptying into the Puyallup river, which in turn in a few miles poured its accumulated water into the tide water of the Puget Sound, I have seen the salmon so numerous on the shoal water of the channel as to literally touch each other. It was utterly impossible to wade across without touching the fish. At certain seasons I have sent my team accompanied by two armed men with pitchforks, to load up from the riffle for fertilizing the hop fields."
> —Puyallup Valley farmer (non-tribal)

1940s–50s: Indian veterans returning home from World War II take veteran's loans and seek to join the non-Native commercial fishing fleets, but due to the cost of equipment and unfair buying practices, many Indians are unable to compete in the lucrative deep-water fishery, and many return to their canoes and nets along the rivers, harvesting fish for their tables.

1950s–60s: Tensions reignite as salmon catches decline rapidly due to a long history of overfishing by non-treaty fishers, and the instillation of dams. Tension among treaty and non-treaty commercial fishermen rise as fish stocks dwindle. Tribal poachers are tried in the media as the culprits responsible for disappearing salmon. The practice of fish and game wardens arresting treaty fishermen resumes. The cases are overturned in federal court, and the state devises a strategy to stop Indian fishing by confiscating nets and boats, upon arrest. By the time a case goes through the state courts, and is finally overturned by the federal courts, fishing season is over. Concurrent with these activities, non-tribal commercial fishermen begin the practice of shooting resident orcas, whom they also see as competition for their profits.

1963: A group of tribal members staged their first protest at the Washington state capital in Olympia. They carried signs that read "No salmon—No santa." After hearing their complaints, Governor Rosellini dismissed them, saying, "Nice to hear your problems. Come back again."

1964: Tribes stage a "fish-in" to protest the unlawful arrests by the state. Marlon Brando joins the cause. A Nisqually fisher and Brando paddle out to the center of the river and lower a net in plain sight of a fish warden. Brando is let go on a technicality in order to not draw attention to the case.

1966: Tribes conduct research on fisheries statistics and release the following finding publicly: 4,500 non-Indian commercial fishermen take an estimated 80 percent of the salmon in the sound before the runs return to the rivers where the Indians fish. These numbers cause a shift in public opinion.

1966–69: Fish-ins continue, and police brutality escalates.

1970: "The Great Tacoma Bust" brings matters to a head, when more than 600 officers participate in a bust in which several Indians are badly beaten. A bystander captures several photographs, and airs them for a full half-hour on the *The Dick Cavett Show*. Public outcry urges the Nixon administration to file a lawsuit to protect the treaty fishing rights. The U.S. State Attorney takes the case after being gassed at a tribal encampment during a fish-in.

1971: Indian fisheries activist Hank Adams is shot point-blank in his car by a white sportsman who called out, "This will teach you damn Indians," upon firing the gun. Hank survived but was briefly accused of shooting himself and asked to take a lie detector test. When he requested that outside witnesses be present to hear the results, the request was relinquished.

1974: Judge Boldt rules that tribes are entitled to 50 percent of the annual catch. In 1974 the total harvested by treaty fishers was only 12 percent, while state departments deliberately oversold the number of licenses, increasing purse-seine licenses by 32 percent and gill net licenses by 53 percent.

1974–present: Due to a severe decline in fish populations, treaty fishers have reduced their fleets to only a few boats, and tribes have taken up conservation efforts to restore the salmon habitats and foster the smolts of struggling populations. In retaliation against the Boldt Decision, several treaty fishers are targets of aggression and intimidation from non-treaty commercial fishers. Tribal students experience increased violence and mistreatment in public schools as the result of hostilities expressed in non-treaty fishing families.

2002: Lummi Nation issues an emergency application for funds in response to the Pacific Northwest Fishing Disaster. The grant application cited, "What is occurring is more than an economic dislocation. It is also part of a cultural dislocation that began over 150 years ago. In 2002 it is finally possible to foresee a Lummi Nation where a majority of its members are not involved in fishing for their basic livelihood. This means both economic and cultural changes that have been effectively resisted for nearly 200 years must finally be addressed."

2013: An injunction is issued, ordering the state to remove obstructions to fish passage and replace the culverts with the most adverse impact on fish by 2030. The order is upheld in the Ninth Circuit in 2016, and the ruling is affirmed by the Supreme Court in 2018.

The Lummi Aquaculture

1919: A non-Native buys a tract of land on the Lummi reservation, and claims ownership of adjacent tidelands. Lummi challenges his claim and the courts rule in Lummi's favor.

1930: A similar claim is made by a man named Stotts, and again the ruling is made in Lummi's favor, referring to the presidential order that established the reservation and gave the shoreline to the tribe, and not the individual.

1931: Lummi goes to court a third time to protect its shoreline when a claim is brought by a man named Boynton, who argued that the shifting shoreline had given him a section of beach because the water had intruded on his property lines. The court again rules in Lummi's favor.

1967: Lummi learns of plans to locate a magnesium-oxide reduction plant on Lummi Bay. Lummi rejects the plan and proposes an aquaculture, with use of their tidelands as shellfish beds.

1969: The Economic Development Administration grants Lummi $143,220 to begin research and training on the aquaculture.

1970: The EDA grants Lummi an additional $1.5 million to complete the project.

1971: The aquaculture pond is completed.

1972: A large shellfish hatchery is built in the style of a traditional cedar longhouse. At present it produces 100 million seed oysters a year.

Notes:
1. From Shakespeare's "Sonnet 29," "And trouble deaf heaven with my bootless cries, ..."
https://www.poetryfoundation.org/poems/45090/sonnet-29-when-in-disgrace-with-fortune-and-mens-eyes.
2. Promises made by Washington Territorial Governor, Isaac Stevens at the signing of the Treaty of Point Elliott in 1855, between the U.S. government and Native American tribes.

"As long as the rivers run, as long as the tide flows, and as long as the sun shines, you will have land, fish and game for your frying pans, and timber for your lodges."
https://harvardlawreview.org/print/vol-135/indigenous-interpretations/

Desire in the City of Subdued Excitement

THE TOWN I GREW UP IN IS CALLED BELLINGHAM. We call ourselves Bellinghamsters, and we have an official slogan, "A refreshing change," but our unofficial slogan is much more fitting. We are the City of Subdued Excitement. Desire is a type of excitement! Here in Bellingham, we subdue all that.

I recently watched an *SNL* skit where two middle-aged mothers were asked what they wanted for Christmas. They let loose their hearts' truest desires (grandchildren). The joke was that it was a refreshing change for a middle-aged woman to be asked, for once, what she truly wished for.

A Christmas wishlist can reveal much about a person's desires. My husband wants a featherweight tent and other odds and ends for motorcycle camping. He desires to ride his bike off into the sunset to camp and do man stuff alone in the wilderness.

My daughter, who is working on becoming a chef and recently severed her thumb tip while chopping chives, has three different types of sharpening stones on her list for Santa. She desires frighteningly powerful tools. She assures me that the sharper the knife, the less likely you are to slip and cut yourself.

A pair of black cowboy boots are at the top of my Christmas list, followed by new blush, beaded earrings, a kettlebell, and cute workout clothes. I desire to be a blushing and physically fit cowgirl.

The boots: My intense desire to own these boots is entirely irrational. That I should want something so extravagant and frivolous surprises even me. But I do. I want them. I desire them. I will wear them with my bar-star Stetson and pretend that I am from a place with sunshine and tacos, a place where cowgirls go two-stepping to three-chord songs about heartbreak and ruin in honky-tonks with handsome, good-timing cowboys.

There are surface longings and then there is their source. My desire for these boots springs from a longing to belong to a carefree and privileged group that represents everything I am not. The opposite of a cowboy is an Indian woman. I exist in the aftermath and ruin wrought by cowboys.

Call it cultural appropriation. I want to dress up and play at cowboy culture. I desire the power available in the kind of self-assurance represented in the cowboy legacy of the American West. The kind of self-assurance required to swagger in, take what I want from this world, and feel 100 percent entitled to it. Entitled to do genocide. Entitled to cause the extinction of people, their customs, cultures, food sources, extinction of lifeways, extinction of entire populations of fish, animals . . . fuck 'em all. If I want it, I'm takin it. If you're in my way, you can get the fuck out or die. Howdy, y'all. Yeehaw!

That's what these 500-dollar boots represent to me. Do you think I'm terrible for wanting that? Are you white? Do you live on stolen land? I'll relinquish desire for the boots and all they represent if you relinquish the maimed and battered Western Hemisphere that was taken and passed down by way of the kinds of attitudes and activities described above.

I live on stolen land. But the stolen land I live on was stolen directly from underneath my ancestors 167 years ago. I pay a mortgage on a house built over the top of a village site that I'm told was burned to the ground after the Treaty of Point Elliott was signed in 1855 and my ancestors were forced to move to the reservation.

That was eleven generations ago. My mother has a photo of herself with her great, great-grandparents, a fifth-generation photo. My daughter can sit in my mother's living room and see back seven generations through that photograph. The great, great-grandparents in that photo were the great-grandchildren of the first people to live within the confines of the Lummi reservation.

When I share the untold history of this region, the response from individuals of European descent is sometimes a retaliatory history lesson of how the Romans colonized the English or the English colonized the Welsh, Irish, Scottish, etc. They want me to relate to their suffering. They seem to say, *it's just the way of the world. Oh well, too bad, better luck next time.*

I see this type of response as attempted denial of the continued oppression of Indigenous peoples by the dominant culture of which the lesson giver is a part. Don't resist. I know it's hard. Try not to be agitated by what I'm saying. Agitation is a form of excitement. We subdue that. Just sit with it. See if it changes you inside. See if it changes your heart's desire.

I grew up on our reservation. In the Treaty of Point Elliott, the reservation is identified as being located on the island of Chah-choo-sen. Diverting of rivers turned it from an island into a peninsula, but it becomes an island again when it floods.

There is an actual island nearby called Lummi Island, on which only two Lummi tribal members reside. The rest of the 903 inhabitants are rich white people and hippies. They speed through the reservation to get to the ferry every day in the hours between 6:00 am and midnight. The road to the ferry was built through reservation land and cuts a straight line through the middle of my family's allotment, which was done without my grandfather's consent. We've lost many family pets to ferry traffic. Other families have lost children.

As a child, I lived on the eastern shore of the reservation. Our house sat atop a hill overlooking the bay. Across the bay sits the town of Bellingham and a portion of the usual and accustomed fishing, hunting, and harvesting grounds of the Lhaq'temish people. That's the real name of our people, *the people of the sea*. We are called Lummi because of a mistake and assumedly because it's easier for white people to say.

I always felt some deep, inexplicable desire to be on the other side of the bay. I thought then that the desire grew out of boredom from the emptiness that filled my days. I think now that I wasn't bored. I know how to entertain myself, and did back then. I think my DNA was restless and lonesome for the days when Lummi people roamed freely throughout the region, and Bellingham was only *one* of our many village sites.

We traveled to different sites throughout the spring, summer, and fall. We followed fish runs and staple crops on a tour through the straits. In the winter, we hunted game and fowl and hunkered down in the longhouses to enjoy the bounty of our harvests. I think I would have liked that life. Going with the flow, always feeling part of it. Instead, I have drifted from job to job, apartment to apartment, working hard to keep my head above water. Trying not to drown in an economic system that doesn't value people and wants their labor to be as cheap as possible.

For many years my heart's truest desire was to be able to one day buy a house in the lettered streets neighborhood of our town. I desired a little house for my daughter and me. A place to be safe and cozy—a house she could grow up in and have fond memories of, maybe even a rope swing. Until her junior year in high school, we lived in a studio apartment downtown, and she had to walk to school past encampments of the unhoused. She walked alongside a creek where her friend's dad found a dead body while jogging.

That creek is the creek for which the county is named: Whatcom. Xwot kwem: xwo = water, kwem = strong. It is the place of strong water. It is where my ancestors brought the first white men who arrived on their shores. The ancestors thought they were going to carry out a great endeavor with these men. They likely didn't realize that these people didn't see them as people, let alone partners. They couldn't have known what plans these white men had for the future.

Before that moment in history, my ancestors fished, lived, and were happy along that creek in their village for thousands of years. I live five blocks away from that creek now. There very well may have been a little summer shack belonging to a Lummi family here on this plot at some point in the past.

When I married my husband, we went shopping for houses in the lettered streets. The first house we looked at was on B Street. It was built in 1910, only 55 years after the signing of the treaty. The house had been in the owner's family for several generations, and had only ever been sold one other time, in the 1930s at a very cheap price.

This means that if we'd purchased that house, the generational wealth attained by the owner who benefited from my ancestors' displacement would be paid out again by me. Because my ancestors were Indians and not cowboys, I pay double, plus inflation, plus the pain caused by knowing the manner in which it was all stolen.

White people inherit houses and stolen land. I inherit heartbreak and intergenerational struggle.

I harbor an aching and persistent desire to write without all this baggage. I really wish I could write love poems, and things to make people feel nice so they'd love me. But people are always asking me how my heritage influences my work and I have eleven generations of paradise-lost to contend with. It makes writing kinda suck a little bit. It's not pleasant material to work with and it's nothing anyone really wants to hear. Nobody likes to bear bad news, but bearing it alone is even worse.

If you stop reading, you leave me here alone with the baggage of our shared history, just like white people have been doing to Natives for 500 years, abandoning their own story—turning away and disclaiming responsibility when asked to make things right. You're better than that. Stay. Listen.

I desire to be treated and thought of in a dignified way without having to overcome stereotypes in people's minds. I desire not to have to work twice as hard to be seen as half as worthy. I desire not to have to worry about any of this.

When I was a child, the first boy I ever kissed broke up with me suddenly for no given reason. Don't worry, I got over it and nobody expects anything less of puppy love. But years later I learned that when we were kids, his father coached basketball and would drive the Native players home to the rez after practice. The boy would ride along, and no doubt noticed how the reservation was different from where he lived. Was this tour of the reservation the cause for his sudden change of heart toward me? Having seen the conditions of some of our homes, did he think of himself as a greater and I as a lesser?

My brand-name clothes, bought from the rez "shopper" who acquired them with a five-finger discount, couldn't fool anyone who'd actually been to the rez. We keep boats in our yards and in some places let the grass and blackberries grow wild along driveways and ditches. But zoom out. We are fisher people. We have been harmoniously fishing these waters for millennia. We have boats; and nature is a fine landscape artist. We have no historic obsession with making fools of ourselves by trying to imitate aristocracy. Perfect green lawns and trimmed hedges are a fashion that was established by lords and ladies in England in the 17th century (and at the detriment to the land's health).

Wealthy landowners relied on servants to tend their lawns. At some point, the servants acted on their desires to keep tiny lawns for themselves. Today, Americans waste a ton of water and effort to maintain their little green patches. The saying "The grass is always greener . . ." establishes the green lawn as the pinnacle of happiness for which one should strive, the mark of civilization.

One should always desire to have the absolute greenest grass so that anyone looking over the fence will be covetous. We should desire to have others desire what we have. Thus is the nature of the lawn and that saying about how green the grass grows.

Everyone in my family is colonized by the lawn concept. They all tend a lawn. The massive environmental destruction wrought by lawns began with someone's desire for a vast expanse of green grass. What if we desired something else that costs less and doesn't take any work? The lawn seems to be something from which there is no going back. It's the same way with many things. Plastic shopping bags and landfills, for instance.

I remember a time in school when a conversation about the rez came up at the lunch table.

"I hear they dump their trash in the street," said a little white girl, who was Jehovah's Witness.

"Is it true? Does your family dump their trash all over the road?" the other girl asked.

"Heck no!" I said. "We burn our trash." I said it with pride, as though we were doing our part to keep things tidy. Both girls giggled.

"You burn your trash?" the Jehovah's Witness asked with disgust. As if her people didn't believe that human beings should burn in hell like trash for all eternity if they dared to celebrate a birthday.

We didn't always burn our trash. We only did that if we had more than a trash bag full before we could make a run to the dump. Why hadn't I just said we take our trash to the dump? Because I thought of the dump as a shameful and disgusting place, while a fire was just a fire? She'd made me feel so small and ashamed, thinking of all the times that I'd stood over the burn pile, making sure that nothing blew away to catch anything else alight.

I didn't elaborate on any of this to those girls. As often happened throughout my school days, I realized I'd made a terrible social misstep. It was a feeling I had become familiar with in my dealings with the white kids. These kinds of experiences had led me to believe that I'm a socially inept person.

"Why don't you just pay the trash man to pick it up?"

I shrugged my shoulders and kept silent.

"Don't you know that there's a hole in the ozone layer?"

I'd heard this but didn't really know what it meant. I just knew that they said my stepsister's Aqua Net was having a bad effect. For the rest of that recess, I sat quietly as the other girls talked, and this became the pattern of my life. Later that night I asked my mother when I got home, "Mom, why do we burn our trash? Why don't we pay the trash man to come pick it up?"

She was making dinner and she laughed at me and said, "Don't be dense. The trash man won't come out to the rez. They don't come here because they say Indians won't pay. I don't know how they know that since they've never tried, and we pay them enough to drop our trash at the dump." She sounded bitter and then finally she asked sharply, "Why?"

"Because the girls at school say there's a hole in the ozone layer and we shouldn't burn our trash."

My mom smiled and said, "Well, those girls are dense if they think that just because someone comes and picks up their trash it magically disappears. Listen to me now. This world and all the pollution—*we don't make it.* The fish don't make it, the clams don't make it, the berries don't make it, and nothing we were doing here before they got here was putting a hole in the ozone layer. We just use their trash along with everyone else because they took away our ability to live in a balanced way. Now don't worry about what those ugly girls say. Just focus on getting good grades."

To be ugly meant to have bad feelings and behaviors toward other people. My schoolmates often revealed their ugliness, and I grew up to understand that if I desired not to be ugly myself,

I would always be on the outside looking in. It's a painful kind of isolation. It's perhaps an even more painful kind of belonging. Since leaving the rez, I've been to plenty of ugly places and survived. These days I'm willing to indulge in a little bit of ugliness, just enough to fit in and enjoy a pair of sexy cowgirl boots.

In some ways it's an adapt or die situation. People who spend their lives on the outside looking in die of demoralization. My brother died of grief over the lost salmon fishery that was tied up so tightly with his identity. He'd been fishing with my dad since he was seven. I think he believed that he would always be a fisherman and when he saw the fishery dwindling away, he dwindled away with it. I remember at his funeral hearing his friend Clara say, "Some people have too soft a heart for this wicked, wicked world."

My stepsister died of grief over her murdered mother. A motherless child is vulnerable and people can sense it. I remember how she would tell me about how the boys at school would stick their hands in her pants or up her shirt while she stood at her locker. She was upset one day because a boy actually put his fingers all the way inside of her. She told an adult. Nothing was done.

She was very pretty and had developed young. She was in C cups by the time she got to middle school. She had a best friend named Patsy. Patsy and Tess. The boys called them Pussy and Tits. Tess tried to giggle about it. I know how it made her feel. Both my brother and sister died trying to make their pain stop. Brother of an overdose, sister of kidney failure. This is a hard thing to know. I myself have tried suicide: straight up once by taking a cupboard full of pills, and indirectly many times by disappearing into the oblivion of drink to see if I would emerge sober or vanish to the other side. I don't do that anymore. I desire to live. Maybe this is the afterlife.

Why tell you all this? Here you thought you were going to read an essay about desire. But if you ever ask an Indian about their heart's desire, don't be surprised if they say something about *Land Back—land back the way it was*; the way it was before the white people came with their Jesus and boarding schools and plastics and *The Great White Father in Washington*.[1] This type of answer is probably why everyone takes such care not to ask us.

Before the colonizers came here, the weavers kept adorable white wooly dogs. Their fur was soft and was spun together with goat's wool to make blankets. The Hudson's Bay Company exterminated the breed in order to sell blankets to the Indians.

Before the colonizers came, there were staggeringly abundant salmon runs and herring spawns. Between 1882 and 1973 the canneries harvested the fishery to near extinction. Tribes were forced to watch in horror from the shoreline as our fishing villages and reef net sites that we had been promised in the treaty were crowded out and replaced by fish traps and canneries.[2]

Prior to the Boldt Decision, tribal fishers were not allowed to participate in the fishery in their own territories. When the treaty fishers were allowed back out on the water, they were given separate openings from the non-treaty fishers, the cowboys. Tribal fishers called them cowboys because during those early days after the Boldt Decision they behaved with hostility toward the tribal fishers, like they were playing the role of cowboys in the old cowboy and Indian movies. They were angry about having to share with people who weren't white.

Tribal fishermen recall the violence and tension at the harbor in those days. They recall being shot at from houses along the shore while they set their nets. After a verbal altercation on the docks, someone set my dad's boat on fire. Another time, someone slaughtered a pig and hung it from the boom of a tribal fisher's boat, insinuating that he was being piggy after making a big catch.

The fishermen knew this was coming when they fought for their right to fish. Previous generations had fished in protest of the unfair laws that kept them off the water. Their nets and canoes were confiscated by the Washington Fish and Game Department. In 1882 a canoe would have been the equivalent of a car or a horse to a tribal family. A canoe was also more than that. Canoes were living beings.

They were thought of as the continuation of a tree's life, having moved from the land to the water, the way a caterpillar moves from the land to the air when it becomes a butterfly. The tree retains its spirit. To have it confiscated meant losing someone who was close to you, someone who chose you as the being they would carry on their existence with. I desire to live in a world that honors that relationship.

I know a white poet who shares a poem about his great-grandmother who was an early colonizer in Montana. He calls her a pioneer and talks about her bravery in settling a hostile and unknown landscape—about how she had to be self-reliant in order to survive.

It takes everything in me not to call bullshit and tell him that she wasn't self-reliant, she was relying on the bounty and abundance of the earth. She wasn't alone in a hostile landscape. There were Indigenous peoples living there for thousands of years before she arrived. Perhaps she didn't know it though, because they lived there in a low-impact kind of way. Would it have killed her to learn those ways instead of insisting on her own way—a way that responded to the world as one responds to hostility, by stamping it the fuck down?

No. The settlers didn't settle anything. They unsettled it. Before they came, there were abundant forests and berry patches, there were lots of fish and animals, and the animals had autonomy. They lived out their lives according to their own aims and purposes, and people lived by teachings that acknowledged their place in the web of interconnection. I desire to have it be this way again. It would be a refreshing change.

That's all the desire I've subdued for now, and now that it's written, perhaps one day, it will be so. Perhaps this desire will take on a life of its own, become even more popular than the lawn. Skoden. Stoodis.

Notes:
1. https://indiancountrytoday.com/archive/woodrow-wilson-the-great-white-father-now-calls-you-his-brothers. https://www.merriam-webster.com/dictionary/Great%20White%20Father.
2. https://casetext.com/case/united-states-v-alaska-packers-assn-1.

Love in the Time of Blood Quantum

SOMETIMES I SPEND A LOT of mental energy worrying about accidentally loving a white man. You may have seen that meme of a bride in a veil with a stunned look on her face and the caption says, "When you were just playing around, and things went too far." That's a little bit like what happened. I did not know it was possible to fall so far so fast in love.

I was internet dating, and then I met this man who I would describe as dapper. He is crisp and tidy, has jacked abs, but is also soft and warm and smells so good, like a man version of the perfect sugar cookie. All I ever want to do is curl up in his smell forever. But also, like a sugar cookie, he is white.

When we met, he worked in the Yukon at a copper mine. That he worked as a high voltage electrician in the Yukon was manly and sexy. That he worked for a copper mine was cringe, but then he'd say, "Where do the fossil fuel protesters think they're going to get all that copper for the engines in their electric cars?"

At that time, the biggest reading I had ever given was at an event called "Keep It in the Ground!" It was all about Indigenous peoples' opposition to fossil fuels and extractive practices. I was on the fringes of all kinds of activism back then but was never sure how any of it could make headway against the mainstream.

His solution to this feeling of helplessness against the current flowing in the wrong direction is to be a vegetarian. When we first met, if I talked about extractive mining, he would talk about how meat and dairy production, besides being cruel to animals, is one of the worst industries worldwide in terms of environmental destruction. Then he would recite all the facts to defend vegetarianism as the number one most effective thing a single person can do to stem the tide of climate crisis.

His feelings about cows resonate with some of my beliefs around food sovereignty, considering how cow feces in river runoff have destroyed the best ancient clam beds in my homelands. (Alas, I love ice cream and cheeseburgers.) He showers at least twice a day (part of the reason he smells so damn good), and when I pointed out that he showers a lot, he said, "I could take twelve showers a day and still not use the amount of water it takes to make a single cheeseburger." I looked into it. He's right.

When we first started dating, there were so many contradictions in how I felt about him. On the one hand, he is a white, atheist vegetarian who doesn't watch football. The whole idea of him would rankle my parents. On the other hand, he's a white, atheist, vegetarian, who doesn't watch football. I could have him all to myself, and my parents couldn't sway him against my own inclinations to do as I please. I always sensed from him that he would always be on my side. I asked him once, "Will you always be on my side?" He said yes.

At the copper mine, his shift was two weeks on, two weeks off. During his two weeks off, he would spend almost every day with me. He would bring me coffee in the morning, and it would be on my bedside when I woke. I would thank him, and he would ask me what I wanted to do that day. Then, as now, he was always sweet, attentive, and kind, but in hindsight, I realize that he was waking me up because he was tired of sitting alone and even though he was easing the blow with coffee, the fact of the matter remains that if he didn't bring me coffee, wake me up, and ask me what I wanted to do with the day, I would have still been doing it. I would have been sleeping in.

Back then I worried that this seemingly harmless act of bringing me coffee was no more than thinly veiled selfishness. Was it a red flag? Turns out, no. He's just an early bird. His people are from the Old Order Mennonites (Amish adjacent), so I always thought his habit of rising before the sun was a sweet character trait he'd inherited, together with pacifism and a ridiculously strict work ethic.

He once showed me an aerial timelapse video of Mennonites doing a barn raising. They looked like ants. I wonder if he looks nostalgically at that lifestyle in some ways, like I look back at the self-sustaining lifestyle my ancestors were forbidden from practicing. But then he tells me how when he was a boy, he and his twin brother went to stay with his grandparents every summer, where they were put to work all day, every day. Once he even had to help his grandfather slaughter a cow. He thinks the experience contributed to his vegetarianism. (He also did an electrical job for a pig farm. He said it was the nastiest place imaginable. "Hell on earth," he said.)

After only a few months of dating we started to get serious, but while he was away in the Yukon I would always be overwhelmed with fears. What if I don't really like him that much? What if he's not who he seems to be? What if I love him? What if I love him, and because I prioritize my relationship with him, I grow apart from my community because he's white?

What if he's like other white men I've loved, and he takes me to the cleaners emotionally, spiritually, financially, and leaves me crying on the side of the road? Maybe the lesson from those experiences is that if you're being tormented and then you get left on the side of the road, but the torment stops, don't cry. You're better off. Historically, partnering up with a xwenítem never ends well for the Indian. Of this, I'm aware.

I recently read a court hearing transcript where Lummi tribal members are rejecting the paltry sum of $57,000 that the federal government decided was fair payment for hundreds of thousands of acres of land given away to homesteaders before the treaties were signed. The oldest to youngest came forward to testify in their own unique way, that the Federal Claims Commission could take its insulting offer and stick it.

One man named Frank Abbot testified. I liked how he talked. He said, "When I see this $57,000.00 I have to laugh . . . Let me say it symbolically: I went and looked at Isaac Stevens' grave and found it. I found him facing downward. He was ashamed after signing those treaties . . . And I say, refuse the forked tongues' allotment as an insult to my people. Refuse the offer. The virgin timber, the abundant game, the Solchuck teeming with fish, it was all stolen by the white eyes." This Lummi ancestor really just says it.

White men are not to be trusted, but damnit if I haven't been fooled every time.

I have the faith of a fool and tell myself, maybe this one will be different. We're at the seven-year mark, and it seems to be going okay so far. I still love the way he smells, and I love it that if I'm really crying, like in real pain, he cries with me and holds me. He cried when he learned about the war in Ukraine. He cried with me after my book was rejected for the twentieth time and I said I wanted to give up writing for good.

I love it that he's a very shy and private person, but he married a poet. Like, did he not realize that his whole life would be fodder for poems forever, to be shared with anybody? I love it that he thinks I'm funny, and when I tease him, he laughs or teases me back. I love it that he never says it, but I can tell he likes the way I look when I wear a pretty dress. Oh yeah, and he's Canadian, so he makes good poutine. (Yes, poutine. Get your mind out of the gutter.)

I could go on listing all the things I love about him, but he's still white, and no matter how much wood he chops (he chops a lot of wood), or how sweet he is (he's very sweet), or how many family gatherings he goes to (not that many), there will always be a huge part of who I am that I will have no way of sharing with him.

It might be my own insecurity, but I can't help feeling like people in my community look at me sideways because I married a white man again, especially after the last disaster. Not only that, but because the federal government doesn't want to own up to the treaties, they instituted blood quantum so that we would become less Indian by half every time we reproduce outside our tribal rolls. So now we carry a CIB (Certificate of Indian Blood) that declares our pedigree like a dog or a horse. They're waiting for us to dilute our way to zero.

Resistance to all genocidal activities and policies is a cultural value. I remember being little and hearing my aunts and uncles talk about being "full-blooded Indian." They said it with such pride that even at the age of three or four, I understood the value of our tribal identity. When

I was returned to my mother, I told her that I, too, was a full-blooded Indian. "Oh, you are not," she said.

"Yes, I am." / "Are not." / "Am too."

"Nope." She said, "You're one-fourth Greek. Your grandpa Bill is a full-blooded Greek."

I had never heard the word "Greek." Since I didn't know what she was talking about, I was at a disadvantage.

"Nah, uh." I said, thinking maybe she was Joshing me.

"Yep." She raised her eyebrows and nodded knowingly. So that was that. I conceded, saying, "Well then, my toes can be Greek." And this story of my response became family lore.

Mothers keep track of bloodlines. When my mother was young, her parents arranged opportunities for her to spend time with a young man from a neighboring tribe. My grandparents got along with the boy's parents and felt he would be a good match for my mom. It didn't work out, but that was how it was done in my mother's generation.

When I was a teenager, my mom tried to provide a similar opportunity for me to date a local Native boy with whom I had no blood ties. It was awkward AF. The truth is, I'm related to most men on my rez, so there weren't many options for me at home, and I never wanted to move to a different rez, like some people do. Also, I was single for five years, and very few Lummi men came forward to ask me out. They came in this order:

1. a super-hot guy twelve years my junior,

2. a decent-looking man twenty years my senior,

3. a nice and very cultural man whose mother is too difficult to abide as family, and

4. a sweet, age-appropriate guy who I liked but who was still under the thumb of his baby mama; oh yeah, and he had a kid, which is fine, but I was almost done raising my own and I didn't want to be roped into a step-parent role.

Even though in five years only four men from my tribe even came close to asking me out, I still felt like a traitor when I started dating a white guy. The truth is, I have never had a real relationship with a Native guy. In school, I was always the quiet, boobless, nerdy girl, and the Native guys were never impressed.

Before I met my current husband, I had been out a few times with a Tlingit guy. One sunny day in June, we were at my tribe's annual water festival, and I was introducing him to my friends and family. We could tell they wondered who he was to me. One of my aunties asked if I was pregnant and eyed him suspiciously. "Nope. Just fat." I said, and he laughed at me. Auntie shook her head.

After we walked away he said, "You should introduce me as your Tlingit husband." We laughed together because we knew that we were not a match like that. But we remained friends for many years. A year or so after the platonic nature of that relationship was settled, I met my Canadian husband.

Now, here I am, like I said before, spending a lot of mental energy worrying about accidentally loving a white man and looking like a naïve Indian girl who says stupid shit like, "Not all white men . . ." and then having doubts because I've just watched *Killers of the Flower Moon* or read something about serial killers, or the crisis of Missing and Murdered Indigenous Women, or history in general.

What the hell is wrong with me? I wonder. Why can't a Native guy love me? Am I a defector? But then, I consider the numbers. Federally enrolled Natives make up less than 1 percent of the American population. Take out half accounting for gender and sexual preference. Then, take out another huge swath for age incompatibility. Finally, take out all the he-hoes who just want a snag, and all the solid guys who are already in relationships, and you have like maybe one guy. And he's probably somewhere in the Aleutian Islands pining away for his Russian Orthodox neighbor lady who he thinks he's not supposed to love.

So that settles it. Love is love and love is good. I was listening to Isabel Wilkerson's book *Caste: The Origins of Our Discontents* and she was talking about miscegenation laws and how interracial marriage was against the law in many states for decades. These laws were enacted to maintain the caste system in which whites hold all the power.

Wilkerson points out that if you are in a loving relationship with someone, you can't dehumanize them. Therefore, a loving, interracial relationship is a threat to the oppressive power structures that deprive America of any chance at a full and beautiful expression of humanity. So, there. Our love is a threat to oppressive power structures; it is a full and beautiful expression of humanity. I like it.

"The poetry of earth is ceasing never . . ."
Reflections on Ecopoetry

AFTER I BECAME WASHINGTON STATE'S sixth poet laureate and the first from an Indigenous community, one of the questions I was often asked was if there is a word for "poem" in my tribal language. I had not learned it, so I went to my teachers, who said, "Well, it could be a sxwiam, a story; a stilem, a song; or a tiwielx, a prayer." I loved this answer because in our culture we know that one needs three things to be sturdy enough to thrive in hard times: stories, songs, and prayers. Poetry is all three, and indeed it has carried me through many hard times.

During my past two years of service as our state poet laureate, I have visited with people from all walks of life and have encountered many attitudes toward poetry. Most are sincere and full of gratitude for an opportunity to be creative and engage with the world beyond textbooks and spreadsheets, but there is always, without fail, a nonbeliever, an individual who thinks what we are doing here with this "poetry" is charming, sweet, and utterly superfluous. Understanding the power of poetry as something essential is perhaps why I am most put off by this attitude.

I suspect that people who are dismissive of poetry are made uncomfortable by its veracity. It's true, many poets I know come off as charming and sweet but we are warriors, scientists, and healers. We are here to say what would be rejected if expressed in ordinary words. We are here to burrow through the layers of emotional sediment accumulated around the fragile ego of humanity. Sure, we're also here to talk about crickets and the unceasing poetry of the earth, but you should know that means talking about death and birth, love and wounding, capitalism and ecocide, climate crisis and extinction.

In poetry, we are here to talk about living—and not just to talk about it, but to connect with life and one another. What I am trying to say here is better said by others who have written before me, particularly the Indigenous Canadian writer Lee Maracle: "We regard words as coming from original being—a sacred spiritual being. The orator is coming from a place of prayer and as such attempts to be persuasive. Words are not objects to be wasted. They represent the accumulated knowledge, cultural values, the vision of an entire people or peoples. We believe the proof of a thing or idea is in the doing."[1]

Here, amid a polar vortex, a wildfire, a hurricane, a heat wave, or a flood, it is perhaps difficult to feel like poetry could save us. Perhaps because we call on poets for eulogies and consolation as we sift through the ashes, we are missing their role as storytellers, bearers of cultural values, and builders of the world. The word "poetry" comes from the ancient Greek word meaning "to make." A poem is offered as a means of understanding the world. If we agree on our understanding, we are making reality. This is powerful. It is the results of the actions we take together, "the doing," that will be the proof of the world we have agreed upon.

Poetry, while precise, relies on metaphor and celebrates connections. It honors individuality while simultaneously embracing alternate perspectives. This makes it an ideal tool for bringing people together in conversation around difficult topics. Talking about ecological disaster will divide a room quickly, whereas ecopoetry invokes a feeling for what is at stake. It can serve as a powerful call to action around which people can unify.

There is a poem that I love by Louise Erdrich called "Advice to Myself."[2] The whole poem is a glorious crescendo to this perfect bit of advice:

> Recycle the mail, don't read it, don't read anything
> except what destroys
> the insulation between yourself and your experience
> or what pulls down or what strikes at or what shatters
> this ruse you call necessity.

Is this an example of ecopoetry? Yes, I would say so. It demands we rethink what we have previously deemed necessary. Beyond that, I would even say that all poetry is ecopoetry because we are ecology, and addressing what separates us from ourselves and the world around us is necessary. I was recently in Las Vegas, where amid all that glitz and excess, I was thinking about how the human suffering brought about by the climate crisis grows more dire every day, and yet how inappropriate a buzzkill it is to talk of such things in a city like Las Vegas (and really pretty much anywhere). One instinctively recoils.

In Las Vegas, it becomes clear that the climate crisis gets so little attention because climate action offers no titillation, no high. Facing reality is the opposite of winning at the tables, the opposite of drinking your face off and leaving your regrets behind at the airport. The ecocide that happens in Vegas stays in Vegas, and the whole world is a metaphor for Vegas, and we are always lifting off into the air, watching our excesses vanish as we climb to thirty thousand feet.

So where do we talk about it? Of course, science and prose are important tools for measurement and sharing information, but how to make meaning of it when there is so much resistance? How can a pie chart that visually represents our level of complete screwed-ness incite action? How can another grim news article light a fire under our feet?

Have you ever been so overwhelmed that you were on the verge of passing out? I recently learned this is caused by strain on the vagus nerve. There is more to it, but one thing that helps calm the vagus nerve is singing. Remember, in my tribal language, a poem is also a song. A song is medicine for when reality is too much to cope with. It's all very scientific.

Globally, we are very sick. We need a doctor with an inspiring bedside manner. We need someone to administer bitter medicine with compassion. We need this person to tell us we're dying while also demanding, "Tell me, what is it you plan to do / with your one wild and precious life?"[3] To whisper assurances like a prayer, "The Poetry of earth is never dead."[4]

Notes:
The title of this essay, "The poetry of earth is ceasing never...," is from the poem "On the Grasshopper and

Cricket" by John Keats, https://www.poetryfoundation.org/poems/53210/on-the-grasshopper-and-cricket

1. From *Introduction to Indigenous Literary Criticism in Canada*, eds. Heather Macfarlane and Armand Garnet Ruffo (Broadview Press, 2015), p. 62, https://broadviewpress.com/product/introduction-to-indigenous-literary-criticism-in-canada/#tab-description.

2. Louise Erdrich, excerpt from the poem "Advice to Myself" from *Original Fire: Selected and New Poems* (HarperCollins, 2003).

3. Mary Oliver, "Poem 133: The Summer Day" from *New and Selected Poems* (Beacon Press, 1992).

4. John Keats, op. cit.

Saving the Salish Sea Salmon

AN ALARMING FACTOID has been floating around for a few years now: In a "business as usual scenario," by 2050, plastics will outweigh fish in the ocean. This figure was first presented at the World Economic Forum in Davos, Switzerland, and is based on a study released in 2015 by the Ocean Conservancy. It says something about plastics, but it also says something powerful about our current inefficacy in fisheries management.

One might easily assume that certainly, the role of fisheries management is to manage habitat and harvest to keep the fishery healthy and productive in a way that sustains it in perpetuity, right? Count the fish, count the fishermen, maintain awareness of stressors, and respond accordingly. With sound scientific management strategies in place, all should be well.

But the fish have been in perpetual decline for over a century. In the Salish Sea, some salmon runs have gone extinct; others are critically endangered. Environmental stressors go unchecked, while economic pressures placed on harvest management create a void in political goodwill to address the problems that face our once-abundant fisheries.

Salmon farms stationed throughout wild salmon migratory routes are breeding grounds for sea lice and pathogens released into migrating salmon populations as they make their way to the ocean. Warming rivers create hostile conditions for adult salmon returning to spawning grounds, while hydroelectric dams present a hurdle for juvenile salmon returning to the sea. Every step in their life cycle is rife with challenges.

A study by the National Oceanic and Atmospheric Administration showed that only 52.5 percent of migrating juvenile spring Chinook survived the journey through all eight dams and reservoirs on the lower Snake and Columbia Rivers. This survival rate is startling on its own, dismal when you consider that Chinook salmon are listed as a critically endangered species.

An important detail in the story of colonization, as well as in fisheries management, is that Western science knows best. We embrace its wisdom for all of the advancements we've made and congratulate ourselves for having left superstition and mythology in the childhood of our evolution. Yet, with all of this good science, why do we find ourselves in a moment of planetary crisis, where ecosystems face collapse, and keystone species are disappearing?

Indigenous scientist Dr. Leroy Little Bear offers this: "Western science is largely aimed at exploration, Native science is aimed at sustainability." It's pertinent to mention that one primary motivation of Western scientific exploration and discovery is to find resources to exploit for economic gain.

In 1883 Thomas Henry Huxley, the president of Britain's Royal Society, addressed the question, "Are fisheries exhaustible? That is to say, can all the fish which naturally inhabit a given area be extirpated by the agency of man?" His scientific exploration of this question yielded the answer: "nothing we do seriously affects the number of the fish." The result of this declaration was that lethal new fisheries technologies were applied, and harvests went unchecked for the next forty years. It was temporarily lucrative for the industry and permanently catastrophic for the fisheries and the Indigenous peoples who historically relied on them.

As part of Huxley's legacy, in Bellingham, Washington, the former home of the world's largest fish cannery, an environmental sciences college is named for him. People in Bellingham are trying to rename a bridge that is named for a confederate soldier, but nobody ever questions the name of the environmental college named for a man whose scientific opinion enabled the plundering of our oceans. If exploitation of resources is the result of science aimed at exploration, what does science aimed at sustainability look like?

Dr. Little Bear gives us this: "If you look at things from a flux point of view, imagine your geodesic communal spider web in motion. Okay, you begin to see that everything is related... In Western thought, we try to isolate. We try to get down smaller and smaller and smaller and isolate, whereas in Native thought, it's always holistic thinking—it's always about the relational networks."

Until now, I have spoken to you as a disembodied voice, given you scientific facts isolated from my personal history and biases. Here, I break the fourth wall. I want to connect with you, invite you into holistic thinking, make you a part of my relational network, and speak to you from my identity as a member of the Lhaq'temish Nation, for whom the devastation to the fishery has been tragic.

Bellingham, Washington, is situated on our ancestral homelands, and we have been historically shut out from practicing our way of life since the mid-1800s. As part of a relational network, from which we've been displaced, this exclusion is a shattering of a web.

A recent study shows that a spider's web is part of its consciousness. A spider uses its woven filament to interact with the world. Every minute vibration is sensed and accommodated for. A breeze, a bird's song, or an ill-fated fly will send ripples through the silk to the middle where the spider sits, senses, thinks, and responds. When it's windy or when the web is heavy with rain, the spider will slacken the lines to release tension and maintain the strength and integrity of the web, its home, its extended body.

Similarly, when people use tools, the brain recognizes the instrument as a part of the body until we release it from our control. Our body is the home of our consciousness. The world is the home of our body. Everything is connected. We connect our consciousness to tools the way a spider is connected to the vibrations of prey and the subtle rhythms of the world that shimmer through its web.

Likewise, in Lhaq'temish culture, we were integrated with the web of waterways and landscapes of our homelands through thousands of years of interactions. We were in resonance with the systems on which we relied. The evidence of this is in how we practiced stewardship in our harvesting methods, and how our stories acknowledge the sacred in the other beings with whom we share our world.

As an example, I'll tell you about the sxwole (shwala). Today, it's known as a reef net because it works by creating an artificial reef. Migrating fish swim up through a manufactured tunnel of grasses and over the false reef into the net. It's a unique technology that collects no bycatch and was traditionally made of willow withes. Because the fishery was tied to a rich cosmology, it was managed with regard for the fish as sacred.

The sxwole was modeled after the way nature creates human life. The sxwole is a womb. Fish swim into the net to give the spark of life to the people for another season. Because women were the net weavers, the reef net was also an essential factor in how we arranged ourselves as a matriarchal society. Each woman who contributed a panel of net secured a share of the catch for her family, and in doing so, secured the esteem of the people.

Colonizers who tried to appropriate the technology had no feel for it and were deterred by the communal effort involved. They wanted a technology that afforded opportunities to secure the profit for themselves, without having to engage other people, and so the reef net became the regional model for early fish traps, which were soon honed into a means of mass-harvest, as witnessed in this passage:

> "Then he began to reminisce and talk to me about the trap days when Bellingham canneries were so loaded that they couldn't can them, and they used to dump as high as 30,000 fish. They just couldn't do anything with them so there was dead fish all over."
> —Jim McKay, Lummi Chief, 1970s tape recording

There was no mythical transference to the fish traps, no communion, no bringing together of minds and hands, no gratitude to the spirit for the gift of life. The traps were eventually outlawed in 1934, but the damage to the fishery had been done and fishing rights were not restored to tribal fishers until 1973. When tribal fishers returned to the water, reef net sites were all occupied by non-treaty fishers. Hydraulics replaced the strength of men. The intricate, glittering web of interconnection had been shattered, and the new story told by the people of the sxwole has become one of survival and repair. We repair by connecting.

I recently learned a new word: *Proprioception*. It is "perception or awareness of the position and movement of the body." I learned the word in relation to dogs. It turns out dogs tend to be mostly front-wheel-drive. They are not as conscious of their rear legs as their front, and this can cause hip problems later in life. As a modern society, reliant on Western science to inform our understanding of the world, we exclude all but observable reality from what we can know. In this, we are a bit like dogs, somewhat unconscious of what our behinds are doing.

Luckily, dogs can learn "rear-end awareness" and avoid problems down the road. People can too. We can learn how to physically interact with our world in a way that acknowledges the unseen and the sacred in each other—people, animals, waterways—and in seeing we can learn to live in non-destructive ways.

Reciprocity in the Age of Extinction

EVERY YEAR MY TRIBE, THE LUMMI NATION, located in the Pacific Northwest corner of Washington State, hosts a First Salmon Ceremony to honor the return of the first salmon of the season, the spring Chinook. This ceremony is conducted as an acknowledgment of the reciprocal relationship between people and salmon. We are told the story of Salmon Woman, who saved us from starvation by sacrificing her children to nourish the people. The story contains the values and practices that uphold our sacred obligation to care for and respect the salmon for their sacrifice.

We honor the first salmon according to custom. We sing songs and offer prayers. Each person in attendance is given a piece of the fish to eat. We are instructed to put the bones aside to be collected and returned to the sea. This is done so the salmon can swim back to Salmon Woman and tell her that we have honored her gift and that we are carrying the sacred relationship forward to the new generation by telling her story and following her instructions on how to care for the fish:

"Never waste salmon. Offer gratitude and never turn your nose up to their gift. Practice respect and care for the rivers and waterways they inhabit. Acknowledge the rules, such as never bathing in areas where salmon spawn or dumping waste of any kind into rivers. Only take what you need. Let nobody go hungry while the catch is being shared. Never abuse the gift, or it will not be there for the people in the future."

The story and its instructions teach us how to be in resonance with the laws of nature. By acknowledging our obligation to follow certain rules that govern a delicately balanced ecosystem, we are practicing reciprocity.

Since ancient times the practice of reciprocation has been a powerful cultural force throughout the world. It is only very recently that, as a global species, we have stopped practicing equal give-and-take relationships with the planet's nonhuman communities and adopted a one-way relationship of extraction to serve the shortsighted interests of a select few. I believe the shift was caused by our turning away from localized nature-based beliefs to adopt homogenous, patriarchal religions, which established a hierarchy that places men at the top with all other life on the planet subjected to their whims and existing for their exclusive use and benefit.

We started calling trees, and fish, and animals "Natural Resources." That allowed us not to think of them as having their own autonomous purpose. They became commodities over which we are guided by divine edict—or, among secular people, by force of custom and assumed human supremacy—to exploit.

Think of *Inter caetera*, the papal bull of 1493, under which the doctrine of discovery was established. Think of Manifest Destiny. Think of any legislative act or court decision upholding the rights of corporations over the rights of people and animals to have access to clean water and a healthy environment.

In 1880 John Waller and the Alaska Packers Association destroyed a Lummi fishing village that had been in use for millennia. They forced the fishers to leave using threats of violence. In 1895 Lummi filed a case against the Alaska Packers Association in an attempt to uphold our treaty rights to fish in our usual and accustomed fishing grounds.

The village was a source of social and cultural exchange, as well as a place to harvest sustenance in accordance with a contract of reciprocity with the natural world, which would allow the community to be fed by its abundance into perpetuity. Nets were woven with willow bark and people harvested in a manner that involved no bycatch or destruction to surrounding landscapes or waterways.

The Alaska Packers Association saw an opportunity to partake in this bounty, and rather than honor the laws of reciprocity, they displaced the Indigenous fishers and usurped their village site to be used as the new location for a canning facility. Environmentally friendly Indigenous harvest practices were replaced by the installation of fish traps that caught humpback and pink salmon as well as Chinook.

In 1897 the court ruled against the Lummi, saying the treaty had not been violated. "It is not competent for this court to interfere by an injunction with the fish traps of the Alaska Packers' Association," decreed the court, "which are authorized and licensed by the laws of the state. Let there be a decree dismissing the suit, without costs."

In a 1972 interview, Ronomus Lear, a Lummi elder, recalls an incident that he estimates to have occurred in 1913:

> "When I was really young, the traps owned by white people would take in all the fish, but they dumped their humpbacks, the pinks. They just dumped thousands of them and they were dying since they had been kept in the traps for so long; they drifted to shore and died. They had the whole Legoe Bay just covered with dead fish. After they drifted away the rocks were still oily from the fish. The rocks would shine on the beach and they smelled like hell. God. Just thousands and thousands of dead fish."

At this time, Indigenous fishers were not permitted to harvest fish, and many worked in the canneries that had displaced them from the waterways and our ancient way of life. It must have been a spiritual blow to see our sacred food treated in such a way. In 1934 the fish traps were outlawed, but by then the fishery had sustained wide-scale devastation and the practice of overfishing had established deep roots in our region.

Too often, the science of fisheries management favors economic gain over ecological reality, resulting in a decline in fisheries worldwide. Rather than a science guided by laws of resonance and reciprocity, we are guided by a science of exploration and conquest, motivated by discovery and extraction of resources. Even worse, the innate human drive to honor the law of reciprocity is used to manipulate us into giving up our rights to clean water and a healthy environment in exchange for whatever compromise is on offer.

The science of social psychology has identified a powerful negotiating strategy called the "Reciprocal Concessions Procedure for Inducing Compliance."[1] It operates on the understanding that if you are offered something and you refuse, and then you are offered something in compromise, you are more likely to meet the compromise as an offer of your reciprocation. You might be familiar with it in retail settings where it is widely used to inflate the price that we're willing to pay for something by establishing a wildly expensive price point for the most desirable item, thereby making the middle-range item seem reasonable.

In the case of how we relate to nature, we are told that clean water and a healthy environment are much too costly. For example: "Oh, so you want a healthy fishery? Do you want to limit harvest, forgo hydroelectricity, and prohibit development to preserve habitat? No? Well, okay … How about we install a very scientifically sound fish hatchery operation and you can have hydroelectricity and catch all the fish you want?" It seems like a good deal.

And that's the system we are in right now. That is the very scientific system by which we are trading away our ability to live on this planet without extirpating other species or driving them to extinction.

The science that governs hatcheries is the same science that was implemented over 150 years ago to serve the interests of hydroelectricity. It is based on weak evidence of efficacy and has operated as a substitute for the sound science of conservation and habitat protection. It has allowed for excessive use of hydroelectric dams and overfishing and has not made good on the promised returns. But we continue to fall for it—to accept the thing that we don't really want in order to reciprocate the compromise offered by power companies, canneries, polluters, developers, and politicians.

The spring Chinook, whom we Lummi honor in ceremony, face the threat of extinction. The Southern Resident orcas, icons of the Salish Sea, our relations under the waves, whose primary food source is the Chinook salmon, face the threat of extinction. It is estimated that up to one million species are threatened with extinction within decades. Globally, Indigenous cultures are faced with losing knowledge and lifeways that connect them to their lands and waterways through sacred bonds of reciprocation.

Are we ready to let it all go in order to hold on to a belief in man's place at the top of a hierarchy that requires no gift in exchange for the gifts of the natural world? Are we really ready to let it all go to avoid sacrificing anything at all in exchange for the sacrifices of Salmon Woman and her children? To avoid acknowledging the sacrifices of beings who die every day so we can live?

I say we should splurge; decline the compromise and instead make sacrifices in order to buy ourselves the nicest most beautiful and expensive item on offer: a sustainable and resonant relationship with our fellow creatures and this glorious living Earth.

An industrial fishery, and indeed industrial-scale production of animals for human consumption, is not sustainable. It relies on the myth that you can have something for nothing. The Law of Conservation of Energy states that "Energy cannot be created or destroyed, only transformed."

Over the last century, we've transformed a lot of life-giving energy into carbon. It's going to take more than technological innovation and creativity to restore balance. It's going to take a transformation of our most deeply held beliefs.

In order to muster the willingness to enter into respectful, reciprocal relationships with nature, we must get something back for what we give, and what we get must feed our spirit as well as our bodies. In the Salmon Woman story, what we get is the gift of gratitude for salvation from starvation. What new story will nourish us in this way? What new powerful story will be the catalyst of our transformation?

Notes:
1. https://web.mit.edu/curhan/www/docs/Articles/15341_Readings/Influence_Compliance/Cialdini.et.al.Reciprocal.Concessions.Procedure.1975.article.pdf.

A Captive Orca and a Chance for Our Redemption

On August 8, 1970, Tokitae was one of six juvenile orcas abducted from the waters off Washington State. Boats, planes, and bombs were used in the hunt and resulting capture, and five orcas died. Juveniles were separated from their pods and netted off to await transport into captivity at amusement parks. During those weeks between capture and transport, the adult orcas never left the abduction site, and the sound of their grief-filled keening rang through the cove.

When Tokitae arrived at the Miami Seaquarium on September 23, 1970, she'd already been named by the veterinarian who oversaw her capture and transport. In Chinook jargon, Tokitae means "Bright day, pretty colors." But in the 1960s, Miami began rebranding itself, marketing itself as a destination with "subtle sex appeal," and Tokitae was given a new stage name: Lolita.

It's believed that the character Lolita in Vladimir Nabokov's notorious novel of that name was inspired in part by the story of a real girl—11-year-old Sally Horner—who was abducted in 1948 and driven across the country to be exploited and abused by her captor. Horner's nightmare ended with her escape after 21 months in captivity. She died in a car accident two years later, but I imagine she was happy to have those years of freedom—a chance to live as a normal teenager.

The scientific name for the orca is *Orcinus orca*. In Latin, *orcinus* means "kingdom of the dead" or "belonging to Orcus," god of the underworld. In the Lummi language, orcas are called Qwe lhol mechen, "Our relations under the waves." To my tribe, the Lhaq' temish of the Salish Sea, they are people. In our stories, they have societies and a culture similar to our own.

They are the first harvesters of salmon, and, like Coast Salish tribes, they are matriarchal. Most remain by their mothers' sides for their entire lives. The matriarchs are the keepers of the wisdom —the decision-makers, the leaders on whom the survival of their pods depend. Lolita's mother is presumed to be a 91-year-old L-pod matriarch known as Ocean Sun.

Serious observation of orcas only began in the 1960s. In 1971, as head of marine mammal research at the Canadian Department of Fisheries and Oceans, Michael Bigg, a Canadian marine biologist, conducted a census, which ultimately found that, at most, there were only 350 orcas left. Previously, it had been assumed that regional orcas numbered in the thousands. The census was prompted by the increased interest in orca capture for display in marine parks. Between 1962 and 1973, at least 47 southern resident orcas were harvested from the British Columbia and Washington coasts; at least 12 orcas died.

Since then, scientists have broken northeast Pacific orcas into distinct types: residents (fish and squid eaters), transients (mammal eaters), and offshore (shark and other fish eaters). Lolita is from the L pod—the largest of the southern resident sub-pods, though only 35 L-pod orcas survive in the wild. The endangered status of the southern resident killer whales has placed them at the center of a fight to restore health and habitability to the Salish Sea bioregion. Their world is a mirror for our own: What happens to them happens to us, and, today, they are facing extinction.

I arrived at the Miami Seaquarium on a sunny Saturday in December, during peak tourist season. I wanted to see for myself the whale I'd read so much about, and the place where she has spent the last 49 years.

I surrendered $51.35 for a ticket and made my way toward the orca arena. The area was shuttered by metal roll-up doors, and the wide concrete hallway was devoid of other patrons. A walk through the rest of the park revealed that it was just as sparsely populated: Vendors stood idle at concession counters, waiting to sell dipping dots or French fries. Grade-schoolers on a class trip splashed about at the underwater touch tank. At the penguin exhibit, an elderly couple stared into the display window, viewing penguins that stood listlessly in the 80 degree heat. Nearby, two children, completely oblivious of the penguins, played with their stroller.

At the edge of a concrete ditch, I leaned against a rail. When I looked down, I noticed two giant sea turtles swimming in the shallow water. One of the turtles swam toward me, bumped into the wall, turned and swam away. When he reached the other side, he bumped into the wall and turned back again. Swim. Bump. Swim. Bump. I wondered if he had been swimming in circles and bumping into walls all day. Or maybe all day, every day, for decades.

As I wandered through the park, I realized the most astonishing thing about the place wasn't the captive wildlife. It was that on this beautiful waterfront, in this coveted real estate market, in this era of enlightened consumers, Seaquarium continues to exist at all. Miami tourism has come a long way since Lolita's arrival at Seaquarium in 1970.

As the world's busiest launch point for cruise ships, the port of Miami is undergoing a $1.5 billion-dollar upgrade designed to create a lush new experience for visitors. The weekend of my Seaquarium visit, the port welcomed 52,000 visitors in a single day. Meanwhile, a few miles away at the Convention Center, Miami Art Basel drew an estimated 83,000 attendees. Hundreds of galleries there paid upwards of $12,000 for a booth. Chic parties and elegant artist's receptions continued deep into the night in stylish Miami Beach hotels and nightclubs.

The bustle of well-heeled world travelers in a shining seaport, the haughty glamour and celebrity of high art—it all stands in stark contrast to this relic of entertainment: an aging whale in a crumbling theme park.

For the first 10 years of her captivity, Lolita shared a tank with a male orca named Hugo. Hugo exhibited what scientists call "stereotypy," a kind of compulsive behavior induced by confinement. He repeatedly bashed his head into the side of the tank until he eventually died of a brain aneurism. The pool where Lolita has spent most of her life—where she watched Hugo die —is 80 feet long by 35 feet wide, with a depth of 20 feet. Lolita herself is 22 feet long. In the wild, orcas dive to depths of several hundred feet.

If I wanted to understand Lolita's world in an objective way, I needed help. At a conference for college mathematics teachers, workshop participants were given the tank's dimensions and asked to measure it to human scale. Answers ranged from 130 square feet to 170 square feet.

How big is that? Think of an area rug 13 feet long by 10 feet wide. Now imagine spending 10 years there with another person. Then 39 more years there with two toddlers.

"This is just making me horribly sad," said one participant. "Is there anything that's in place to try and get her a bigger home? Or is this just her life forever?"

"What's the standard captive killer whale tank size?" asked another.

"It's supposed to be at least 48 feet wide," I explained.

Minimum standards require that a captive whale must be able to swim twice its length in any direction.

"So it's not even legal," said another participant.

Debate about Tokitae's tank has been ongoing for more than a quarter of a century. In the 1990s Washington Governor Mike Lowry and Secretary of State Ralph Munro launched the "Free Lolita!" campaign. In 2003 animal rights activist Russ Rector called on officials to issue code violations against the park.

In 2005, due to their rapidly dwindling numbers, southern resident orcas were granted protection under the Endangered Species Act. In 2015 the act's protection was specifically extended to Tokitae. It was hoped that the law would mandate her release. Instead, her endangered status worked against her, with some claiming that freeing her would make her vulnerable to "serious harm." In September 2017, Hurricane Irma struck Miami, forcing the evacuation of 6.5 million people. Seventy-five people died. Lolita was left behind.

An orca's brain has the tissue and structure necessary to support high-order thinking and complex processes such as language, self-awareness, and consciousness of visceral feelings, like empathy, embarrassment, and loneliness. Orcas are highly social with unique cultures and languages. Tokitae's group, the southern resident killer whales, eat only salmon and squid and live in the waters off the southern tip of Vancouver Island. There are three subpods—J, K, and L—and Tokitae is from L pod.

Each pod has a distinct set of shared vocalizations—a pod song. It's not inherent; it's learned. Tokitae still sings her pod song. After 49 years, she hasn't forgotten.

Pat Sykes, a former Seaquarium employee, remembered Lolita's early days at the aquarium, when she was still just a baby. "The skin on her back cracked and bled from the sun and wind exposure," Sykes said. "She wouldn't eat the diet of frozen herring. . . . At night, she cried."

Throughout history, captivity has been a major U.S. industry. According to Justice Department statistics, since 1970—the year Tokitae was captured—the national incarceration rate increased by 700 percent. As of November 2018, more than 14,000 immigrant children are incarcerated in camps operated by the federal government. Since 2017, at least six children have died in custody, or immediately upon release.

In 1925 more than 60,000 Native American children were removed from their homes and placed in boarding schools. Many experienced treatment tantamount to torture. Many ran away. Some died, trying to find their way home. Between 1879 and 1918, nearly 200 children were buried at Carlisle Indian Industrial School in Pennsylvania. There were at least 150 other such schools in operation during the same period.

A disproportionate number of Indigenous women go missing every year, enough to spark international outcry from tribal communities across the United States and Canada. Many of the women are never found, and some are found murdered. The movement to raise awareness of this horror is referred to as the crisis of Missing and Murdered Indigenous Women. At a recent Lummi Nation gathering, women sang and danced in honor of our lost sisters. Little Lummi girls held signs saying, "MMIW—I'm not next."

If vulnerable people are taken from their families against their will and they die, the charges against the perpetrators are kidnapping and murder. If orcas are my relations under the waves, and if Tokitae dies alone, 3,400 miles from home, and if her body is quietly disposed of after a lifetime of exploitation for profit, are kidnapping, enslavement, and murder the crimes that have been committed?

Because poisons accumulate in their blubber, orcas are more vulnerable than most animals to environmental toxins. Problems associated with chronic exposure to toxins intensify when orcas go hungry and blubber is metabolized into their bloodstream. Toxins are also passed through the mother's milk, but approximately 70 percent of southern resident orca pregnancies are lost due to nutritional stress. There simply aren't enough fish anymore.

On September 25, 2019, the United Nations released a report by its Intergovernmental Panel on Climate Change, which presented the stark truth about rising temperatures, ocean acidification, declining oxygen levels, and threats to crucial marine ecosystems. The impact of all these changes, the report noted, will be felt in increased weather disasters, rising sea levels, the proliferation of pathogens, and threats to human food security.

This grim assessment by the U.N. Panel on Climate Change has one major purpose: It is supposed to influence the decisions of the world's leaders. But those leaders don't seem convinced. Across the Western Hemisphere, Indigenous communities fight to protect our homelands against destructive practices by governments and corporations. But we consistently come up against a different worldview, one that has no interest in protecting salmon or our relations under the waves, doesn't believe in the interconnection of all things, and stands apart from the rest of nature, insisting that humans "have dominion over the fish of the sea, and over the fowl of the air, and over every living thing that moveth upon the earth."

As a species, humans have followed this biblical directive to the exclusion of all reason. There are environmental protection laws, but those continue to place the health of the planet below the health of the bottom line.

Last fall, I went fishing with a Lummi elder—a fisherman with more than 40 years of experience on the water. The boat broke down 20 minutes from shore. As we waited for a tow, a skiff approached us. It was another pair of fishermen—a father and son out since daybreak.

"We're starving out here," said the man. "We only caught one fish."

After accounting for fuel, their take-home pay would be .08 cents. In Lummi culture, a fisherman is esteemed as someone who feeds the people. But this has become increasingly difficult.

After the boy and his father motored away, the elder fisherman sat back in a folding chair and gave a heavy sigh. "'Stick and stay and make her pay,' is what we say. . . . 'Be one of the first ones on the water and one of the last to leave.' Live by those rules and sooner or later you're going to catch 'em. I guess not anymore."

The following story was recorded at Klallam in 1925:

> "These people were blackfish (orcas). They invited him in and gave him something to eat. One day he fell asleep and when he woke he heard people outside the house as though they were lifting something heavy. Then they were quiet. He went out for he thought they had a whale. He saw nothing but a diver. He asked what they were trying to move. They said they wanted to move the whale, but it was nothing but a diver duck. He took the duck by the leg and moved it. They thought he was a great man to be able to move such a monster. They asked him what power he wanted."

This story says two things: First, nature is reciprocal. It will nourish us and give us opportunities to return the favor. Second, if the blackfish want their whale moved, and we move her, they will grant us power.

When I entered the orca arena, I walked up to the edge of Tokitae's tank. She swam close—right up against the wall—and stayed there, suspended at the surface. A couple of Seaquarium employees stood watch, but aside from them, I was alone with her. I sang her a song, and she made vocalizations back to me. Eventually, a noisy school group and other people trickled in. I took a seat to watch the show. Rock 'n' roll blared through the loudspeakers, a young woman in a wetsuit tossed fish into Tokitae's mouth, a video on a Jumbotron talked about how

Tokitae was loved and cared for while her wild relatives were going extinct. I felt horribly sad.

Then, there was a new feeling. Seeing Tokitae there in that tiny pool, knowing she'd spent nearly five decades there, raised doubts. What if returning her to the Salish Sea was the wrong thing to do? Even with the sea sanctuary proposed for her retirement, how would she adjust? I stayed until the young employees told me to leave, but on the way to my hotel, the question split me in two. It was wrong that she was there to begin with, but what if we were wrong on all sides on what to do with her?

I drove out to the lighthouse on Key Biscayne. I rolled up my pants and waded in the ocean. I looked out to the water and asked for an answer. As rarely ever happens, an answer came: In 1970, when Tokitae was taken, the courts didn't see her abduction as a crime. But if the capture was carried out today, the perpetrators would be arrested and prosecuted, and the whales would be released.

We have ended the practice of orca abduction because it is brutal. Now it's time to take another step. If the blackfish want their whale moved, and we move her, they will grant us power, the power to heal our relationship with the natural world.

Note: Since this article was published—in April 2020—Tokitae, the last Southern Resident orca living in captivity, died on August 18, 2023, at the age of 57.

The Pandemic Pages
(excerpt)

4.3.20

I am doing the dishes for the millionth time. And the word "weary" keeps repeating in my head. It catches itself on a lyric. I put on Otis Redding, and he sings to me,

> *Oh she may be weary*
> *Them young girls they do get wearied*
> *Wearing that same old shaggy dress, yeah, yeah*

Us old girls do get weary too. But for now, I have Otis, the dishes, and food. For all this, I'm thankful. I also have TV. Did you know that St. Claire of Assisi is the patron saint of TV writers? How do I know this? I get a little nostalgic for the church every year around Easter. Last month I was looking to go to confession for being so ungrateful, so I went to the website of the local Catholic church. I saw that they were offering classes for people wanting to receive the sacrament of confirmation.

Before this pandemic, I was feeling pretty lost. Confirming my faith in a church I don't attend seemed like the answer, so I started researching patron saints for my confirmation name. Saint Bridgette is the patron saint of poets, but I wanted to find a patron saint of writers. I discovered that St. Claire is the patron saint of TV writers because she had illuminated visions projected against her bedroom wall.

I'm taking this disruption in regular scheduling as a sign that I'm not meant to be a confirmed Catholic, but now at least I know who to pray to for good television and the care of those who write it. It is TV writers who shall shepherd me through this strange time. I've been binge-watching *Lost*. There are 122 episodes, so it'll be there for me for as long as I can stand it. It's about survivors stuck on an island. There's some kind of quarantine, and nobody really knows *wtf* is going on. It's a deeply relatable show right now.

The episode today is one in which the millionaire with a food addiction is hoarding a food supply. He overcomes his demons by dumping his stash, only to find that a massive new shipment of junk food has fallen from the sky. His rare problem is dealing with abundance, while most people have the opposite problem. We're all working through some shit.

There's no more chocolate in this house, and for the first time since all this started, I've had a slight feeling of melancholy. The reality of this pandemic, the hardship that so many have already experienced, seems to be creeping its way toward me, and I may soon find that I have no job. I don't know what this will mean for the mortgage, or my eligibility to sponsor Sparky's immigration, but I imagine it won't be good.

The TV keeps saying we're all in this together. I have an Italian friend who taught me the phrase *mal comune mezzo gaudio*, "a shared evil is half a joy." I realize that the hardship I'm about to experience will be felt by millions. This doesn't bring me joy, but it makes it a little less scary, even slightly hopeful. In tarot, the tower card means something is crumbling so that something better can be built on a firmer foundation. In *Lost*, each survivor of the crash was en route back to an unbearable life. The crash gives survivors a clean slate.

Before the pandemic, I'd never even seen one episode of *Lost*. It aired when my daughter was a toddler and I was an undergrad. I had no time for TV, and I've never paid for cable in all my adult life. "Kill your TV" was a thing when I was young, and I grew up on a reservation where there was no TV unless it could be picked up with an antenna. The choice was *Star Trek* or *Star Trek*, so we watched *Star Trek* and wished that explorers from Europe followed Starfleet's Prime Directive instead of the Catholic Church's Doctrine of Discovery.

Side note: the papal bull that set out the Doctrine of Discovery was called *Inter caetera*, which translates to "Among other things." The church's justification for what was done in the Americas was a mere side note in Catholic lawmaking. Sometimes non-Natives have asked me why Indians are Catholic, after all the injustices done in god's name. Faith is always complicated to explain, but lately, I've come to suspect that my relationship to Catholicism is an intergenerational case of Stockholm syndrome.

Anyway, when kids at school would talk about *Seinfeld* or *Friends* I always wished I had a clue as to what they were talking about so I could join the conversation. (Nobody ever talked about *Star Trek*. Weird, right?)

This is one of the many ways Native culture is different from white culture. You possibly had teen years filled with *Seinfeld*, *MTV*, and images of people in the media who looked like you and affirmed that you were super cool. We had teen years filled with *Star Trek* reruns and the oral tradition—which recounted, and recounted, and recounted our tribal history to us, so that we understood in our bones that we are the children of survivors, and we are also survivors. And our children will be survivors.

Hearing our history is like a vaccine. It contains a deactivated strain of what could kill me. It stings when administered, makes me a little sick, and teaches my cells how to survive. Our songs are sacred food. They give strength to carry that weight of our terrible history, and to soothe the injuries of unprovoked hatred leveled against us.

One passage in the oral history we tell is about a pandemic. Whether by a pandemic of microbes or murderers, 90 percent of the original inhabitants of the Americas were dead within two generations of European contact. It has been called "the greatest demographic disaster in the history of the world." One survivor among nine dead.

People use the word "decimate" to describe catastrophic destruction. The word originated with the ancient Roman practice of killing one in ten men as punishment for the group. I don't think there is a word for nine killed and one surviving. If one in ten is decimation, what is nine in ten? I supposed genocide would be the closest name for it.

The first wave of pandemic swept through our region ahead of the physical arrival of invaders. When the men came in their ships, they came into vulnerable, grieving communities that had been ravaged by disease. In hunter-gatherer societies, there is no such thing as a non-essential worker. Everyone is essential. Starvation followed pestilence. I am a survivor of this history. I still cry over it. I still sing over it.

4.5.20
Farmers are on the news talking about how their crops are not going to get planted and they're going to go broke, while other farmers are talking about dumping product because there's no restaurant market. Still others are talking about how their crops are not going to get picked and are going to rot in the fields because they can't get their workers back from Guatemala and "Americans just don't want to do this kind of work." Meanwhile, unemployment is up 300 percent, and the price of food is about to skyrocket. The news says that hospitals are going bankrupt, and Sparky asks, "How can that even be allowed to happen?"

"Oh, Spark," I say. "You and your socialist medical care. This is capitalism, hon. In god we trust."

4.7.20
Today, I work in the garden and go for a bike ride. After dinner, I drive along the eastern shoreline of the rez, which is the best place to watch a moonrise. I see that dozens of non-Natives have made this discovery as well. They line the roadside with tripods and cameras at six-foot intervals.

I park and watch the sunset cast its shimmering farewell across the bay. The snow on the mountain turns the pink of cherry blossoms, and then, the moon rises. It peeks out, golden from behind the Twin Sisters, casting its reflection in a bright line on the water. When it is clear of the horizon and dusk settles on the bay, I chase the moon into Bellingham, looking for a nice picture of its face above the quiet cityscape.

Seismographers say that the earth has quieted. Whale researchers say a reduction in marine vessel traffic has quieted the sea, causing cortisol levels in whales to drop. This time away from my job has caused my cortisol levels to drop, as well. The bags under my eyes have disappeared, and I feel young and happy again.

Happy enough to ride bikes, write poems, watch birds, and chase the moon. If mother earth were to invent a virus, it would make the earth quiet so the whales could hear each other sing again.

4.8.20

"The birds sang, the proles sang, the Party did not sing." This is a line from George Orwell's *1984.* Another one that gets me is a line by Russell Baker, "We are in the hands of men who make no music and have no dream." I have this chilling realization whenever I turn on the news, so I turn it off and use music as a balm to cheer me. Lately, I want to sing all day. I want to read poems all day. I want to sit and listen to birdsong and silence all day long.

I've been waiting to write until I felt like I have something to say. I keep thinking that things are so redundant around here and, probably, similarly so for everyone else in the world, that I couldn't possibly have much to write worth reading. Then I notice that the birds seem to like a loose branch in my tree that bounces when they land on it. They take turns flying to it and bobbing up and down until it stops. It's like a little birdie carnival ride. They love it. I'm at my window watching them when daughter calls.

The restaurant where she used to work has offered her a few hours doing a deep clean since the dining room is closed. She's calling to ask if I'll bring her some books and her work shoes. I gather the requested items in a paper bag and deliver them. We hang out like cops in a parking lot, talking to each other from six feet away through our rolled down car windows. I wish we had donuts.

We talk about how everything is being done remotely. I tell her about a physicist I saw on YouTube, who explained that every living thing on earth is an organic, remote-data-gathering machine. Like highly sophisticated space rovers, we are trillions of perspectives sending earth's images, sensations, and emotional reactions back to a universal intelligence so that it can better understand itself. Ants send ant perspectives, bees send bee perspectives, the birds send theirs, you send yours, and I send mine.

"Are you high!? You been smoking pot, mom?"

"No," I say. "The other physicist on the video said he believes that we are not remote information gatherers, but little pieces of the universe expressing itself." So, there you go, researchers and artists have their camps in physics too.

I don't realize that my headlights are on, and we talk until my car battery goes dead. Daughter pulls her car around in front of mine, and I hook up the jumper cables, but something isn't right. There is a terrible smell and then suddenly, lots of smoke.

"Take them off! It's going to explode!" Daughter screams.

For a moment, I'm sure I'm going to die of electrocution, but I decide to risk it and pull the jumper cables off. Shaken, I call Sparky, and he rides his bike to where we're parked. He hooks up the jumper cables correctly, and all is well. When I get home, I turn on some music. I watch the birds and wonder if I'm the universe expressing itself, or if I'm sending it something new to consider about the nature of music and love. I think both.

The Secret Medicine

"There is a secret medicine given only to those who hurt so hard they can't hope. The hopers would feel slighted if they knew." —Rumi

FOR A FEW YEARS NOW I'VE BEEN WORKING as a professional writer, and people often look at me with concern and ask, how are you doing, what have you been up to? And honestly, sometimes it's difficult to justify even to myself, this odd routine of loafing about, window gazing, navel gazing, scribbling—it's hard to justify as actual work, so when people ask me what I'm up to, I offer a list of commissions I've accepted, talk about how I'm participating in capitalism like a good little drone.

This thing we do as writers, for some reason, is not regarded as something with obvious value like, oh, say, brain surgery, curing cancer, CPR. However, while it may be less quantifiable, what we do as writers is necessary. I keep thinking of a story shared by an editor I know about how, during the most treacherous depths of COVID, romance novels were her only comfort. Stories are medicine, the secret medicine out in plain sight. By interpreting and reflecting on our experiences, we are always laying bricks on the path to a deeper understanding of the human condition.

There is a famous quote misattributed to the anthropologist Margaret Mead. She is supposed to have said, "The first sign of human civilization is a healed human femur . . . because wild animals would be hunted before their broken bones could heal." She didn't really say that. What she actually said was, "We have called societies civilizations when they have had great cities, elaborate division of labor, some form of keeping records."

While her actual quote resonates with anthropologists, I would say the misattributed quote resonates with writers. To write about the human condition is to be acutely aware of what's been broken and to posit an idea of how one might heal. Sooner or later, life breaks all our figurative femora, and now here we are, all of us trying to hold each other up and care for each other the best we can so that we might survive together, report victories and failures, and tell our stories of hope and despair. Our humanity expressed in fear manifests as poison—greed, aggression, anger. Our humanity expressed in love is the antidote—beauty, art, music, literature.

There's a quote by the author Ben Okri. He says, "Stories are the wisest surviving parts of a people's stupidities or failings." I love that. And if the story isn't entertaining, instructive, or inspiring, then at least, hopefully, we've shared a bit of ourselves and connected, and that's really what we're doing when we tell a story, right? We're connecting. Becoming whole by sharing something of ourselves and our understanding of the world, our humanity. After all, I've heard it wasn't even a healed femur, or cities, or even written records that were the first signs of civilization. It was our ability to tell stories.

Poems were the original way of transmitting story. A poem is a vibration in our vocal cords. It lives on the page, but it also lives on our breath, originally in our memory. The rhymes were the mnemonic device. When we give our human voice to the words, they become a vibration organized in a special way with a cadence akin to music. I was talking to another author recently, and she was telling me that as long as she's singing, she can't get stuck in negativity or worry, and so she sings all the time. This singing has the same impact on the page.

When I was in grad school I took an oral history class and we were visited by an Emergency Medical Technician (EMT) who told us that the first thing first responders try to do is get the person they're treating to tell them what happened. It helps them to process trauma and keeps them from slipping into shock. It also helps them to internalize and understand the details of what happened so that they can process it later with a greater sense of control over the story and their own healing process.

Storytelling is powerful. I believe that storytelling through writing is even more powerful because if writing is thinking and we can change what we write, then we can change what we think.

We can write our way out of negative self-talk and harmful views. We can also use writing to clearly visualize a future for ourselves. It's a powerful tool for shifting perspective. We can zoom in, zoom out. Things look very different when you zoom out. Perspective is something we writers pay close attention to, along with distance and detail.

When I was a Job Skills Instructor, I used to have a series of activities that I took clients through step by step to help them see their prospects from a different perspective. Many of the steps I took them through involved writing down where they had come from and where they wanted to go. At the end of the process, many of my clients were able to find fulfilling employment. After helping one client land her dream job, I thought, wow, geez, I should try this.

I took the assessment that I gave to my clients. I had this big spiel. When people came in, I would tell them that the assessment was linked to a database of more than 50,000 jobs listed in the Department of Labor's register, so there was something in there just for them. Despite this, I never really felt like there was anything there for me. I enjoyed my work as a job skills instructor, but it never really felt like my life's work.

Then one day I came across a poem by the dervish poet Hafiz. He said,

> If your heart cannot find a joyful work
> The jaws of this world
> will probably
> GRAB hold of your
> Sweet
> Ass.

I found that little poem oddly threatening but also reassuring; it implied that there is such a thing as joyful work. What could that be? So, I took the assessment I gave to my clients, and guess what? It said I should be a poet, and that was the day I learned that "Poet" is a real job. It was listed right there in the Department of Labor's database of more than 50,000 jobs, so it had to be. Up until that point, I never really considered that "poet" was a viable career. I had always used it only as a refuge, a place to scurry into to survive, to maintain a sense of self and sanity in a crazy world.

After taking that career assessment, I thought, what the heck? Why not give poetry a real go? I followed all the other steps I used to lead my clients through and within a year, I was named Washington State Poet Laureate. So maybe I'm meant to be a job skills instructor after all.

Anyway, now that I've had the experience of being a professional poet, I realize that poetry is much more valuable and sustaining as a creative refuge, a secret medicine, and I'm trying to find my way back to this little sacred sanctuary in my heart, the creative well from which one draws the sweetest coolest water. I have returned to the poems I love, the ones that made me fall in love with poetry. The ones I've used as spiritual aspirin. Here are a few of my favorites.

Upon Julia's Clothes
—Robert Herrick

Whenas in silks my Julia goes,
Then, then (methinks) how sweetly flows
That liquefaction of her clothes.

Next, when I cast mine eyes, and see
That brave vibration each way free,
O how that glittering taketh me!

"Hope" is the thing with feathers
—Emily Dickinson

"Hope" is the thing with feathers –
That perches in the soul –
And sings the tune without the words –
And never stops – at all –

And sweetest – in the Gale – is heard –
And sore must be the storm –
That could abash the little Bird
That kept so many warm –

I've heard it in the chillest land –
And on the strangest Sea –
Yet – never – in Extremity,
It asked a crumb – of me.

Autobiographia Literaria
—Frank O'Hara

When I was a child
I played by myself in a
corner of the schoolyard
all alone.

I hated dolls and I
hated games, animals were
not friendly and birds
flew away.

If anyone was looking
for me I hid behind a
tree and cried out "I am
an orphan."

And here I am, the
center of all beauty!
writing these poems!
Imagine!

won't you celebrate with me
—Lucille Clifton

won't you celebrate with me
what i have shaped into
a kind of life? i had no model.
born in babylon
both nonwhite and woman
what did i see to be except myself?
i made it up
here on this bridge between

starshine and clay,
my one hand holding tight
my other hand; come celebrate
with me that everyday
something has tried to kill me
and has failed.

It's nice to have a few little songs to cling to. To recite as a reminder that there is a secret medicine, glittering to taketh me, that there is hope on the chilliest seas, that I am the center of all beauty, that every day something has tried to kill me and failed.

So, to writers, artists, musicians, creators of all ilks—next time you have any doubts about why you do what you do and whether it's a worthwhile pursuit, remember, you're looking for a cure for the human condition of believing we are somehow not connected. You're looking for a cure for loneliness—you're concocting, partaking of, and administering the secret medicine.

Flourishing in the Seasonal Rounds

TO MY ANCESTORS, the islands of the Salish Sea were a garden. There is a tenet in anthropology that large complex villages require agriculture. But on the coastlines of my homelands, since time immemorial, without traditional agriculture, we Lhaq'temish flourished. What does it mean to flourish? I think it means that the sun pulls you from the darkness of non-being, bestows on you the gift of life, and calls you forth to brandish all your beauty. If you have ever watched a timelapse of blossoming flowers, you will see that they sway and quiver, then explode like firecrackers, integrating and alchemizing sunshine—releasing it as their own shimmering radiance like light in the darkness.

To flourish means blooming, but it also means that though blossoms wither and fade, if they receive the proper nutrients, they can come back stronger, more plentiful, and more beautiful with each new cycle. I believe the ancestors understood the cycle of flourishing and aligned with it to benefit themselves and all within that radiant circle. I believe this because, for thousands of years, they enjoyed sophisticated foodways, a rich cosmology, and intricate artistic traditions without the toil of traditional agriculture.

In the winter months, they came together in large villages, while warmer months called for travel through the islands to all the beloved places, the usual and accustomed fishing, hunting, and harvesting grounds. Spring root sites, summer fishing villages, fall hunting camps. This way of life, our she'lengen, is known as a "seasonal round," meaning the people traveled in tandem with the harvests, moving with the seasons.

Cultural practices like controlled burns and selective harvesting ensured that the gifts of a particular place would return strong in the next cycle. The relationship to food was a direct exchange between the people and the Earth. There were no faraway factory farms, canneries, supply chains, ocean freighters, or exploited laborers. No grocery stores or cashiers to ask "plastic or paper?" Instead, the people had harvest songs, and as they worked, they sang, while birds sang back from the trees.

The ancestors ate food from the island prairies, forests, and shorelines and accepted the gifts of a fond and loving landscape that poured forth a profusion of nourishment, beauty, and a feeling of well-being and connection. In our traditional diet, omega-3 fatty acids in salmon provide Vitamin D—the sunshine nutrient that insulates people from the gloom of winter. Rose hips and berries give antioxidants, potassium, magnesium, Vitamins C and K, fiber, and prebiotics along with their sweetness. Shellfish give B-12 for vitality and energy. Wild game furnishes protein. Foraged greens and roots give minerals and medicines, and the seasons offer variety, the spice of life.

Every stop in the seasonal round offered new ingredients for the endless feast. Flowers glowed in the landscape like wrapping paper on a gift. When a camas flower blooms, it's your birthday, dig in. Enjoy! Blossoms signal forthcoming berries—all kinds of berries: wild strawberries, black caps, trailing blackberries, salmonberries, thimbleberries, salal, gooseberries, huckleberries, blueberries. In lowland bogs were tart cranberries, and in the trees, bitter red elderberries; each berry type with its own dynamic benefits from boosting immunity to suppressing appetite.

To hunters, the forests yielded deer, bear, and elk, while the sky gave ducks and geese. To gatherers, the landscape offered fiddleheads and the roots of licorice ferns, which chased away a sore throat. Cattail, skunk cabbage, and wild water lilies (in addition to camas) produced starchy roots that could be dried and saved as staples. Miner's lettuce and clover were eaten as fresh greens, while sea asparagus, wild carrot, and onion added complex flavors.

Streams provided clean, clear drinking water, and when the weather was cold, rivers ran with eulachon, whose oil was a welcome warmth, adding umami to the menu. Twice a day, the beaches gave such bounty that the people had a saying, "When the tide is out, the table is set." There were succulent horse clams, butter clams, little necks, cockles, and oysters. Nestled in the seaweed and shallows were tasty Dungeness crabs, octopi, sea urchins, and many other delectables.

In the cold, teeming waters off the village's doorstep, all you had to do was drop a hook, and up would come a ling cod or colossal halibut. Herring ran so thick that the people raked them from the water like autumn leaves. Herring roe was a delicacy to be savored. There were also flounders, dogfish, snappers, and perch. And, of course, there was the keystone species whose generosity sustained all life in the Salish Sea bioregion: the reliable and bountiful seasonal sacred salmon.

> People of the sea sing in gratitude
> with stories of how salmon give themselves
> to nourish the people with sacred food.
> For as long as salmon swim, all will be well.
>
> Grandmother tells how out in the cold straits,
> our most ancient kin, the Qwel lhol mechen
> Sing "this is where the salmon run today."
> Follow the beacon of the tallest fin
> And you shall share in the bountiful feast.
> This is how it was when we were still joined
> in a web connecting greatest to least
> with abundance for all to enjoy.
> We sing to remember our gratitude
> to the life that becomes our sacred food.

Around four thousand years ago, the ancestors devised an innovative technology called a reef net, the operation of which strengthened community bonds. The nets were woven by matriarchs who each contributed a panel to be sewn together like a quilt, ensuring each contributor a portion of the catch. The net was strung between two canoes anchored side by side. It had a hole at the top to allow for escapement. When the captain gave the word, the men in the canoes hauled up the net, and the catch was taken from the middle of the run, allowing salmon at the back to continue with fish at the front. This selective harvest kept the runs strong. The reef net design was modeled after a womb. When salmon swim up the false reef and into the net, they become the spark of life to carry us into a new cycle.

This cycle flourished for thousands of years and might have continued for thousands more, but in 1855 the Treaty of Point Elliott was signed. Despite the treaty's guarantee of access to our usual and accustomed fishing, hunting, and harvesting grounds, we were denied our rights and isolated from the garden—the gifts of our homelands, our beautiful way of life. We still maintain our way of life, as much as we can within the changes brought about through colonization, but of course, the garden is not what it once was.

How did our garden come to be? As an Indigenous writer, I am sometimes asked if I will write about our tribal prehistory. People like to hear our ancient stories. Of course they do. But those stories are not meant to be written. They contain wisdom accumulated over millennia. Their roots are sunk deep in the land and waterways. Those stories acknowledge the living spirit in every plant and animal that lives here. They are like etymology, explaining that *flourish* comes from ancient times and means "to adorn with flowers." While animals are called such because they are infused with *anima*—from the Latin for "spirit," or "breath," perhaps connected to the Greek *anemos*—for "wind." To be animated—animal—alive, is to have breath, spirit. The beautiful flower we call anemone shares its name with the sea anemone, which translates from the Greek as *windflower* or daughter of the wind. This name acknowledges a relationship between the wind of the world above and the wind of the world under the waves.

My ancestors also observed the blossoming of flowers and the shift of the wind. They also acknowledged a relationship between our world and an unseen world under the glittering surface of the Salish Sea, the home of the Qwel lhol mechen, *our relatives under the waves*, also known as Southern Resident killer whales. Because of the unique culture of the Qwel lhol mechen and our ancient relationship with them in our shared homelands and waterways, we understand that their world mirrors ours, we understand that what happens to them happens to us. It's easy to recognize this relationship when you look at the similarities between their culture and traditional Lhaq'temish culture. Like us, Qwel lhol mechen are good at catching salmon. They follow the lead of their matriarchs, and always travel together as a family. They are also known to sing and gather in celebration with neighboring pods. For all these reasons, their name acknowledges our connection, "Our relatives under the waves."

We understand our world a little better by understanding how it is named—how it came to be known. And when we understand something, we are better able to love it. This is what the ancient stories do. They give meaning and anchor us in the world. A long time ago, some say as long ago as twelve thousand years, the glaciers receded, leaving a rocky, barren landscape. The majestic forests had yet to take root, but there was water, clear cold water, and then salmon came, bringing all the rich minerals of the sea in their shining bodies. Everything partook of these riches and began to flourish. The ancestors came down from the Frasier River canyon and made a life in these islands.

Because it's good to understand something about this place and our relationship to it, that you might love and respect it as we do, I will share a Lhaq'temish story that I made into a poem with permission from my Oksale, my teacher. The story is an abbreviated telling of a longer saga. It is not my story. I do not own it, and, as a Lhaq'temish birthright, it is not to be shared without permission from our culture bearers. My version is only an iteration in an ongoing, fluid, and ever-changing tradition. Like others in our oral tradition, this story has flourished—been animated by the breath and voices of many tellers over hundreds of generations across the region.

This is the story of Kwome and Kwelshan,
two mountains in my homelands,
and how, through their parting of ways,
the islands of the Salish Sea came into being.

A long time ago, the mountains were married.
For some reason, who knows why?—
one day Kwome decided it was time
to be on her way.
As she traveled she wept
and her salty tears
became the swirling eddies of the Salish Sea.
Soon, she grew tired and stopped to rest

She set down her texwitch, *her bow*
to have a bit of xwelol, *camas*
and when she got up to go,
in her sorrow she forgot her texwitch,
and dropped a little piece of her xwelol,
these became islands, the people know
as Texwitch,[1] *the island shaped like a bow*
and Pen'nex'weng[2] *the island, where we go*
to p'aneq, *to dig* for xwelol.

She went along this way, leaving gifts
for the the people. And the gifts have stories
to map the bounty of the Salish Sea.

When she arrived where she stands today,
she decided that was far enough away.

Sometimes on a clear day, you can see her
all the way from her old homelands
where once she stood with handsome Kwelshan.

He likes to catch a glimpse of her
glowing majestically in the rare sunshine.
He could look at her and nothing else
for the rest of his life. But soon she decides
it can't go on this way, and she draws the clouds
around her face to disappear back into the gray,

and that is how the ancestors explain,
these blankets of clouds, the falling rain.

In my work, I had an opportunity to speak at an event in Canada. I shared the story of Kwome and Kwelshan. Afterward, a tribal elder (I don't remember which nation) thanked me for sharing. He told me Kwelshan was their mountain too. He relayed a few anecdotes from their stories, and it made me smile to hear the affection with which the elder spoke of our shared mountain.

At a similar event on the WSÁNEĆ reserve in Canada, I noticed that some of their language corresponded to words I know in the Lummi language. The similarities were explained by a tribal elder with the aid of a large map of the Salish Sea. On the map, he circled a traditional Lummi village site out in the islands. Then he circled a WSÁNEĆ village site and drew a line between the two. "Look how close we were," he said. "You could get in a canoe in the morning and ride the current to be in Lummi land by the afternoon."

It was a lovely reminder that we are all connected in ways we may not even be aware. We each are a part of something bigger. We Lhaq'temish have been here sharing this landscape, these waterways with the flora and fauna of the place for a very long time. We will continue to be here for a very long time. As the elders say, our human lives are just the blink of an eye in the creator's timeline. International borders, destruction of habitat, endangerment of species, and other consequences of colonization cannot last forever. Until then, may we seed knowledge of our rich heritage and make our minds fertile ground where a dream of natural abundance can take root in our collective imagination so that together, we might enter a new cycle of flourishing.

Notes:
1. Texwitch, *the island shaped like a bow*: Eliza Island, Whatcom County, Washington.
2. Pen'nex'weng, *the island where we go*: Vendovi Island, San Juan Islands, Washington.

Acknowledgments

DEEPEST GRATITUDE TO Rebecca Mabanglo-Mayor, Phoebe Bosché, Kathleen Alcalá, Phillip H. Red Eagle, and the whole team at Raven Chronicles Press. Hy'sxw'qe to my Sachs, John Ballew and all the ekw'seles in the Xwlemi-Chosen office. Many thanks also to the editors and organizers who supported the creation of these essays, especially Paul Hanson and the Chuckanut Writers Conference; Andre Bouchard at Indigenous Performance Productions; my gracious hosts Duncan and Melany Berry at Skookum Wawa; Erin, Maura, and Katie at Storyknife; Rika and John Mouw, the generous sponsors of the Fireweed Fellowship; Eric Greenwell and Gary Lilley at the Port Townsend Writers Conference; Dustin Renwick and Cheryl Zook at the National Geographic Society; my Fish Outlaws team, Andrea Reid, Lauren Eckert, and Amy Romer; Mary Sutton at Poets.org; John D'Onfrio at Adventures Northwest; Dave and Ilyssa Kyu at Campfire Stories; Margot Kahn, Kelly McMasters, Brandon Keim, Tristan Ahtone, Dayna Patterson, Tiffany Midge, RYAN! Fedderson, and my friend and first reader, Ryler Dustin. You are all forever in my heart for the important work you do in the world. *Ngen'se Hy'sxw'qes!*

Emily Dickinson, " 'Hope' is the thing with feathers," from *The Complete Poems of Emily Dickinson*, edited by Thomas H. Johnson. Cambridge, Mass.: The Belknap Press of Harvard University Press. This poem is in the public domain.

Louise Erdrich, excerpt from the poem "Advice to Myself," from *Original Fire: Selected and New Poems*. HarperCollins, 2003. Reprinted with the permission of the publisher.

Hafiz (1325–1390) excerpt from his poem "A Hard Decree."

Robert Herrick (1591–1674), "Upon Julia's Clothes." This poem is in the public domain.

Frank O'Hara, "Autobiographia Literaria," from *Selected Poems of Frank O'Hara*, edited by Mark Ford. Knopf, 2009. Reprinted with the permission of the publisher.

John Szwed, *Cosmic Scholar: The Life and Times of Harry Smith*, Farrar, Straus and Giroux, 2023.

Isabel Wilkerson, *Caste: The Origins of Our Discontents*, Random House, 2020.

Elissa Washuta and Theresa Warbuton, editors, *Shapes of Native Nonfiction: Collected Essays by Contemporary Writers*, University of Washington Press, 2019.

Credits / Sources

Earlier versions of the following essays, which are included in this book, *Positively Uncivilized*, were published as follows:

"Defenses of Peace in the Biosphere Reserve": Published on the Skookum Wawa website, June 2024, https://skookumwawa. net/residents.

"Fish Outlaws: Reflections on the Criminalization of Indigenous Fishers and Imagining Just Futures": Published on the Fish Outlaws website, June 2023, https://www.fishoutlaws. net/project/essay.

"Desire in the City of Subdued Excitement": Published in *Wanting: Women Writing About Desire*, eds. Margot Kahn and Kelly McMasters, Catapult Publisher, 2023.

"The poetry of earth is ceasing never … Reflections on Ecopoetry": Published in the Fall-Winter 2023 issue of *American Poets*, the biannual journal of the Academy of American Poets.

"Saving the Salish Sea Salmon": Published in *Adventures Northwest*, October 2020.

"Reciprocity in the Age of Extinction": Published in *Nautilus Magazine*, September 2020.

"A Captive Orca and a Chance for Our Redemption": This article appeared in the print edition of *High Country News*, April 1, 2020, https://www.hcn.org/issues/52-4/.

"The Pandemic Pages (excerpt)": Published in *Psaltery and Lyre*, April 2020.

"Flourishing in the Seasonal Rounds": Published in *Campfire Stories: San Juan Islands*, 2025, https://www. campfirestoriesbook.com/books).

Biographical Notes

Rena Priest is an enrolled member of the Lhaq'temish (Lummi) Nation and served as the sixth Washington State Poet Laureate (2021–2023). She is the first Indigenous person to hold this post. Priest is also the recipient of a Washington State Book Award and an Allied Arts Foundation Professional Poets Award. She has received fellowships from the Academy of American Poets, Indigenous Nations Poets, Nia Tero, and the University of Washington Libraries. Her first collection, *Patriarchy Blues*, received an American Book Award. Her second collection, *Sublime Subliminal*, was published as the finalist for the Floating Bridge Press Chapbook Award. She published a nonfiction book, *Northwest Know-how: Beaches*, with Sasquatch Books, and is the editor of two anthologies: *I Sing the Salmon Home: Poems from Washington State* and *The Larger Voice: Celebrating Native Arts and Culture Foundation Literature Fellows*.

Her poems appear in *Yellow Medicine Review, Poetry Magazine,* "Poem-a-Day" at *Poets.org, Verse Daily*, and elsewhere. Priest's nonfiction appears in *High Country News, Nautilus Magazine, Seattle Met, Adventures Northwest, American Poets*, and *Campfire Stories*. Priest holds an MFA from Sarah Lawrence College and lives in Bellingham, Washington. You can learn more at renapriest.com.

RYAN! Elizabeth Feddersen (cover artist) specializes in creating compelling site-specific installations and public artworks that invite people to consider our relationships to history, culture, the land, and our non-human kin. She completed a Bachelor of Fine Arts at Cornish College of the Arts in 2009, and is now based in Tacoma, Washington. Feddersen grew up in Wenatchee and is an enrolled member of the Confederated Tribes of the Colville Reservation, from the Okanogan and Arrow Lakes bands, and of mixed European descent. She investigates creative strategies to activate engagement through interactive materials, community sourced content, social practice, fun, and humor. These approaches enable her work to start conversations about a broad spectrum of subjects and promote collective learning. Feddersen has created large-scale site-specific pieces and interactive installations throughout North America, and has a growing body of permanent artworks in the public realm.

Other Raven Books and Publications

FUTURE X, fiction by Georg Koszulinski
  Paperback, ISBN 979-8-9914032-1-4
  eBook, ISBN 979-8-9914032-2-1

Treasures in Heaven, Raven 2nd edition, fiction by Kathleen Alcalá
  Paperback, ISBN 978-1-735480-6-7
  eBook, ISBN 979-8-9914032-0-7

This Light Called Darkness, A Raven Chronicles Anthology, Selected Work 1997–2005, Eds. Kathleen Alcalá, Phoebe Bosché, Paul Hunter, and Anna Odessa Linzer
  Paperback, ISBN 978-1-7354780-4-3

Poem of Stone and Bone: The Iconography of James W. Washington Jr. in Fourteen Stanzas and Thirty-One Days, by Carletta Carrington Wilson
  Paperback, ISBN 978-1-7354780-2-9

The Flower in the Skull, Raven 2nd edition, fiction by Kathleen Alcalá
  Paperback, ISBN 978-1-7354780-3-6
  eBook, ISBN 978-1-7354780-5-0

Words from the Café: An Anthology, Raven 2nd edition, edited by Anna Bálint, photographs by Willie J. Pugh
  Paperback, ISBN 978-0-9979468-9-5

Spirits of the Ordinary, A Tale of Casas Grandes, Raven 2nd edition, fiction by Kathleen Alcalá
  Paperback, ISBN 987-0-9979468-8-8
  eBook, ISBN 987-0-9979468-6-4

Take a Stand: Art Against Hate, A Raven Chronicles Anthology (Winner of the 2021 Washington State Book Award for Poetry), edited by Anna Bálint, Phoebe Bosché, and Thomas Hubbard
  Paperback, ISBN 978-0-9979468-7-1

Stealing Light, A Raven Chronicles Anthology, Selected Work 1991–1996, Edited by Kathleen Alcalá, Phoebe Bosché, Paul Hunter, and Stephanie Lawyer; Paperback, ISBN 978-0-9979468-5-7

Publisher's Acknowledgments

Raven is indebted to our 2025 Co-Sponsors for partial funding of our programs: the City of Seattle Office of Arts & Culture (Centering Arts & Racial Equity (C.A.R.E.); 4Culture (Sustained Support, through King County Lodging Tax and Doors Open funding). Thanks to all those who donated during the GIVE BIG 2025 Campaign for their generous donations in support of Raven publications and programs:

Crows: Kathleen Alcalá, Frances McCue
Steller's Jays: Susan Deer Cloud
Mockingbirds: Anonymous, Risa Denenberg, Sharon Hashimoto, Richard Simonson, Paul C. Hunter, Sibyl James, Larry Laurence, Joannie Stangeland, Harold Taw, Ronda Broatch
Rooks: Lenora Good, Anna Linzer, John Mifsud, Mary Ellen Talley
Jackdaws: Rachel Beatty, Natalie Pascale Boisseau, Bethany Reid, Susan Pace Kathleen Flenniken, Diane Glancy, Sheryl Sirotnik
Magpies: Rachel Harrington

—Phoebe Bosché
Managing Editor, Raven Chronicles Press

www.ingramcontent.com/pod-product-compliance
Lightning Source LLC
Chambersburg PA
CBHW021653120626
46545CB00002B/842